LIVING WITH
PURPOSE
BIBLE STUDY

Proverbs, Ecclesiastes & Song of Songs

LIVING WITH
PURPOSE
BIBLE STUDY

Proverbs, Ecclesiastes & Song of Songs

A Gift from Guideposts

Thank you for your purchase! We want to express our gratitude for your support with a special gift just for you.

Dive into **Spirit Lifters**, a complimentary e-book that will fortify your faith, offering solace during challenging moments. Its 31 carefully selected scripture verses will soothe and uplift your soul.

Please use the QR code or go to **guideposts.org/spiritlifters** to download.

Living with Purpose Bible Study: Proverbs, Ecclesiastes & Song of Songs

Published by Guideposts
100 Reserve Road, Suite E200
Danbury, CT 06810
Guideposts.org

Copyright © 2025 by Guideposts. All rights reserved.

This book, or parts thereof, may not be reproduced, stored in a retrieval system, or transmitted in any form or by any means, electronic, mechanical, photocopying, recording or otherwise, without the written permission of the publisher.

Cover design by Judy Ross
Interior design by Judy Ross
Cover photo by malerapaso/iStock
Typeset by Aptara, Inc.

ISBN 978-1-961251-31-1 (hardcover)
ISBN 978-1-961251-32-8 (softcover)
ISBN 978-1-961251-33-5 (epub)

Printed and bound in the United States of America

CONTENTS

About Living with Purpose Bible Study 3

An Overview of Proverbs, Ecclesiastes & Song of Songs 7

LESSON 1: PROVERBS 1:1–9:18
The Wisdom of a Well-Ordered Life 14

LESSON 2: PROVERBS 10:1–22:16
The Two Ways: Wisdom Contrasted with Folly 46

LESSON 3: PROVERBS 22:17–31:31
Virtues and Vices 71

LESSON 4: ECCLESIASTES 1–4
The Mystery of Life 105

LESSON 5: ECCLESIASTES 5–10
Futility and Faith 136

LESSON 6: ECCLESIASTES 11–12
Wisdom for Young and Old 162

LESSON 7: SONG OF SONGS 1–3
The Lover and the Beloved 181

LESSON 8: SONG OF SONGS 4–8
Love and Desire: Romantic Love and the Love of God 207

Acknowledgments 235

A Note from the Editors 236

About Living with Purpose Bible Study

For as long as humankind has existed, we have pondered our place in the universe. Poets and preachers, philosophers and scientists alike have explored the topic for generations. Our busy modern lives leave little time for contemplation, and yet we move through our lives with nagging questions in the back of our minds: *Why am I here? What am I meant to do with my life?*

Fyodor Dostoevsky wrote that the "mystery of human existence lies not in just staying alive, but in finding something to live for." You might wonder how living with purpose ties in with the Bible. That's because God's Word is a guidebook for life, and God Himself has a purpose—a unique mission—for and unique to you. Reading the Bible and seeking God through prayer are two of the main ways God speaks to people. And when we begin to seek God, when we pursue His truth, when we begin to live our lives in ways that reflect His love back to others, we begin to find that purpose. Finding our purpose is not a destination; it is a journey we'll travel until we leave this earth behind and go to our heavenly Father.

Most of us know something about the Bible. We might be able to quote verses that we memorized as kids. Many of us have read parts of it, have learned about it in Sunday school both as children and adults. But not as many of us *know* the Bible, and that is where this Bible study comes in.

"Bible study" is a term that can elicit a variety of responses. For some people, the feeling that comes is a daunting sense of intimidation, even fear, because we worry that the Bible will somehow find us wanting, less than, rejected. Maybe we've heard preachers wielding the Bible as a weapon, using it as a measuring rod and a dividing line that separates "us" from "them."

Guideposts' *Living with Purpose Bible Study* addresses these questions and concerns with a hope-filled, welcoming, inclusive voice, like the one you've grown to know and love from Guideposts' devotional books, story collections, magazines, and website.

Best of all, you'll discover that the writers of *Living with Purpose Bible Study* are experts not only in the depth of their Bible knowledge but also in sharing that knowledge in such a welcoming, winning way that you can't help but be drawn in.

The writers come alongside you as trusted friends, guiding you through each volume in that warm, inviting manner that only Guideposts could bring you.

Each volume in the study draws from five trusted translations of the Bible: the New International Version, New American Standard Bible, the Amplified Version, the English Standard Version, and the King James Version of the Bible. We encourage you to keep your favorite Bible translation on hand as you read each study chapter. The Bible passages you read act as the foundation from which the study writer's insights, information, and inspiration flow. You can read along with the writers as each chapter unfolds, or you can read all of the passages or verses included in the chapter prior to reading it. It's up to you; you can use the method that works best for you.

In addition, you'll find two distinct features to enhance your experience: "A Closer Look" entries bring context by presenting historical, geographical, or cultural information, and "Inspiration from Proverbs, Ecclesiastes & Song of Songs" entries demonstrate the spiritual insights people like you have gained from their knowledge of the biblical text. We've also provided lined writing spaces at the end of each lesson for you to jot down your own thoughts, questions, discoveries, and *aha* moments that happen as you read and study.

A final note: Before you read each chapter, we encourage you to pray, asking that God will open your eyes and heart to what He has to say. Our prayer for you is that you find a new or renewed sense of purpose and grow closer to God as you deepen your understanding of God's Word by enjoying this *Living with Purpose Bible Study*.

—*The Editors of Guideposts*

An Overview of Proverbs, Ecclesiastes & Song of Songs

Our studies in these lessons will take us into three uniquely different but equally fascinating Bible books. Two of these books, Proverbs and Ecclesiastes, are classic examples of the writings produced by sages in ancient Israel. The third book, the Song of Songs (or the Song of Solomon, as it is sometimes called), while not directly included among Israel's wisdom literature, does contain a strong flavor of wisdom influence.

Despite their seemingly disparate approaches, these three books share some important features.

Proverbs and Ecclesiastes are both classic examples of a class of literature that probably appeared on the scene during Solomon's reign and continued to flourish after the Jewish exiles had returned to Judah from Babylon. We refer to this as Wisdom Literature. The other examples of this genre in the Old Testament are the book of Job and Psalms 1; 19; 37; 49; 73; and 112.

Ecclesiastes and the Song of Songs share the distinction of being known as festal scrolls. They are two of five scrolls that were traditionally read at the annual feasts of Israel. (Song of Songs is traditionally read at Passover in modern Judaism.) The other festal scrolls are Ruth, Esther, and Lamentations.

The individual themes of these three books can be summarized in this way:
- Proverbs deals with simple assurances and firm warnings. Moral questions are seen in terms of stark contrasts, black and white—little gray.
- Ecclesiastes, on the other hand, acknowledges that things are often not as they seem. Learning and riches are not always signs of God's blessings—they can be empty and meaningless. Ecclesiastes disturbs us with its questions, making us probe deeper.
- The Song of Songs—often called the Song of Solomon—celebrates something that most of us are familiar with: romance, love, courtship.

Another way to look at these three books: Proverbs aims at the will; Ecclesiastes is directed at the intellect; and Song of Songs is written to the heart.

The Book of Proverbs

The book of Proverbs is rich in two- and four-line sayings of practical instruction about life. There is real "down-home" instruction about thrift, attitudes, getting along with people, making decisions, home and married life, success, justice, etc. Contained in the book is a sort of folk wisdom that is made up of small, essentially unconnected, elements, except that it all focuses on a central theme that is expressed by the Wisdom writer in these words: "The fear of the Lord is the beginning of wisdom: and the knowledge of the holy is understanding" (9:10, KJV).

The writer does not focus on basic religious themes as found throughout most of the Old Testament. Instead, he concentrates on what is involved in making sense, as he sees it, out of the ordinary and daily routines and relationships of life.

The Book of Ecclesiastes

The book of Ecclesiastes is possibly one of the most neglected books in Scripture. And yet, as we will find out as we study it, Ecclesiastes can also feel like one of the most modern books because the questions it raises are as relevant today as they were when they were first written down.

The word *Ecclesiastes* translates the Hebrew term *Kōheleth*, which means "one who convenes a congregation," probably with the intent of preaching. You might have heard a form of the word, *ecclesiastical*, used concerning practical matters of the church. For that reason, the speaker throughout is the Preacher.

The Preacher wrestles with deep, relatable questions: What is my purpose? Do the things I do have meaning? Why does God allow the wicked to prosper while good people are cut down in their prime? We see him struggling to learn, freely acknowledging that there is a God in charge of human affairs but at the same time not believing that God's ways can be known and understood by people. And while life's questions can't all be answered while we are here on earth, the Preacher suggests that the best thing a person can do is live life heartily, be happy, and enjoy the good things of life because they are a gift from God (3:12–13).

Although it seems to be disjointed and complex, the book of Ecclesiastes merits our study and thoughtful attention.

The Song of Songs

Unquestionably, no book in our Bible has caused as much speculation as this one. Consequently, a variety of explanations and interpretations have been assigned to it. Whatever else it is, though, we have a superb celebration of human romantic love—one of God's great gifts—in the form of poems that are rich in imagery.

Its acceptance by the Jewish rabbis as official Scripture came only after a great deal of struggle. But around AD 100, a leading rabbi named Akiba gave it his full endorsement by saying, "The whole world is not worth the day on which the Song of Songs was given to Israel; for all the Writings [Scriptures] are holy, and the Song of Songs is the Holy of Holies."

Over the centuries interpreters, both Jewish and Christian, have seen in these love poems allegories that speak of Christ's love for His bride, the church, or of God's love for Israel, but there is no hint of this in the writings themselves. Nevertheless, the early church fathers found it easy to see the Christ and His church symbolized in the love poems.

Of one thing we can be sure—human love is colorfully celebrated in marriage. And the love expressed between the two lovers in the poems may well symbolize a divine love that transcends everything else.

As a part of our sacred Scriptures, the Song of Songs merits our prayerful attention and study.

Was Solomon the Author?

In Jewish tradition, all three of the books in the study are associated with Solomon, who reigned as king during the time the Hebrew people remembered as their golden age—a period of prosperity, extensive empire, far-flung trade, and international influence.

There are obvious differences in tone, style, and subject matter among these three books. Perhaps as a result of these differences, rabbinic tradition holds that Solomon wrote them at different stages of life. According to their tradition, the Song of Songs was composed in his youth, Proverbs was a product of his middle years, and Ecclesiastes was written in the disillusionment of his old age.

The claim of Solomon's authorship of these books comes from tradition, meaning it is an understanding that it has been handed down from generation to generation. Proverbs may certainly have been partially collected under the sponsorship of Solomon's court, and he may have composed some of them himself. But, as you will see as we look at them closely, it seems likely that, as most modern Bible experts believe, they came from more than one source.

Ecclesiastes seems to use Solomon as the "voice" of the book. For example, when we see the words, "I have been the king of Israel," it clearly becomes a literary device suggesting the experience of a person who had wealth, power, and pleasure but who saw them as "vanity of vanities"—empty, meaningless things that occupy our lives but to no good purpose. Who better to have experienced that side of life than Solomon? But we know that there was, of course, no time at which Solomon himself could have remembered his kingship in the past tense (as the Hebrew wording suggests). Instead, we see the writer powerfully invoking the image of Solomon as he examines the futility of all that Solomon possessed to the fullest.

The opening verse of Song of Songs is translated as "The song of songs, which is Solomon's" (KJV) or "Solomon's Song of Songs" (NIV). But the wording in the original manuscripts could be rightly translated as any of the following: the Song *of*, *by*, *for*, or even dedicated to Solomon.

Because he was known for his divine gift of wisdom (see 1 Kings 3:3–28 and 4:29–34), Solomon is seen as someone who possessed keen insights into the well-ordered life and a rare understanding of what it meant to taste deeply of life. Thus, Solomon came to represent a kind of person who was especially important during the period in which he lived and reigned as king of Israel. A person with Solomon's attributes was known as a "sage." We are already familiar with the role played by prophets and priests in the biblical story, but the archetype of the sage—a wise observer of life—came into prominence at the time of Solomon and was a factor in Israel's life and culture from that time on.

These three books carried an important message for the people of Israel, one that is still vital for God's people—us—today. It is simply this: Life, if we look at it long and hard, is not without meaning and purpose. There is a deep satisfaction in a life that is committed to God. He is a God of justice (Proverbs) and love (Song of Songs), and it is through Him alone that we make sense of life (Ecclesiastes). Because this is true, we can follow with confidence the advice of the Wisdom writer, "Trust in the Lord with all your heart, and do not lean on your own understanding. In all your ways acknowledge him, and he will make straight your paths" (Proverbs 3:5–6, ESV).

LESSON 1: PROVERBS 1:1–9:18

The Wisdom of a Well-Ordered Life

◆─────────────◆

Father, be my guide to wisdom. Help me to receive Your instruction with gratitude. Amen.

Adages, aphorisms, witticisms, epigrams, maxims, and axioms: Every society has its stock of wise sayings, thought-provoking questions, and homespun guidelines for living. Early Americans had their own favorites. Some came from the Bible, and others were collected in places like *Poor Richard's Almanac,* published by Benjamin Franklin.

"A stitch in time saves nine." "A penny saved is a penny earned." "Early to bed and early to rise makes a man healthy, wealthy, and wise." These are sayings that have circulated in our language for close to 250 years. They have been copied down by generations of schoolchildren, quoted at the appropriate occasion by adults, and alluded to frequently in literature, drama, and film. We breathe them in like the air, and whether we follow their wisdom or not, they are reminders that a life well ordered is a life well lived.

Fyodor Dostoevsky and Aleksandr Solzhenitsyn frequently quoted Russian proverbs in their writings. Great orators in the English language, such as Abraham Lincoln and Winston Churchill, made liberal use of the short epigram. The bywords and parables of their day were the raw material of dramatists such as Shakespeare and Molière, of poets such as Goethe and Dante, of allegorists such as Bunyan and Swift, of essayists such as Voltaire, of propagandists such as Trotsky and Goebbels, and of preachers such as Luther, Wesley, and Knox.

Just as words and syntax are aspects of our language, so are these brief summary statements that appear like little capsules of thought throughout our writings and our conversations. They help us to communicate because they represent the collected thoughts, the shared wisdom of a culture. No civilization has ever existed that did not—in some way—treasure its common experience in the form of proverbs.

The Proverbs of Israel

It isn't surprising that these sayings or proverbs, so reflective of life and experience, should travel from one culture and language to another. Nor is it surprising that when a proverb is taken into a new society or culture it is reshaped to fit the prevailing attitudes of those who have adopted it.

This was especially true of the people of Israel because they lived at the crossroads of the ancient Near Eastern world. Situated along the Jordan valley and in the hill country to the west and north, the people of Israel were at different times closely associated with Egypt in the south and with the Babylonian and Assyrian cultures that emerged near the Tigris and Euphrates rivers to the east and north.

While the Israelite people were influenced, and even dominated, from the seventh century BC onward by Babylonia, Persia, and Greece, they did not merely adopt the proverbs of these nations uncritically. Instead, they selected them and shaped them in a manner consistent with Israel's own experience as the covenant people of God.

The book of Proverbs is a collected body of a broad range of sayings, many of which had their origin outside of Israel. The fact that Israel saw all of these sayings as possibilities for expressing their own religious experiences and convictions says something important to us.

First, it suggests that a belief in one God—one God for all people—makes us more open to recognize truths that come from other people and other traditions. While the Israelites may have become fiercely intolerant of foreign gods, they learned to embrace the truth even if it came from these foreign sources. If it is true, they reasoned—and so must we—then it comes from the one true God.

Second, this fact tells us that Israel felt free to employ these sayings in a way that suited their own society and culture. The very idea of a sacred Scripture implies that the truths of that body of writings can be applied in new ways, reinterpreted for new situations and for changing generations of readers.

This simply means that the proverbs apply to a wide variety of people and circumstances precisely because they have a common source. So Israel's exclusive devotion to one God made them far less exclusive in their use of the wisdom, the songs, and the literature of other people. God's wisdom is a reality that permeates all the world and its people. Put another way, all wisdom is God's wisdom: "The Lord founded the earth *by wisdom*, He established the heavens *by understanding*" (3:19, NASB, emphasis added).

Consequently, all wisdom leads to God. Wherever wisdom is found, the key that unlocks its secret rests with Him. This thought is always close at hand in the book of Proverbs as, in various ways and in colorful language, the writer emphasizes the eternal truth that wisdom . . . knowledge . . . understanding . . . insight come through "the fear of the Lord," as the majority of Bible translations word Proverbs 1:7.

Finally, the fact that the people of Israel freely borrowed from other nations tells us that these truths are seen as adaptable to differing circumstances. They selected them, shaped them, and used them in ways that were appropriate to their own society and their own experience of God. The very idea of sacred Scripture and of writings that become a touchstone of truth for a people implies that these writings are found to be true in a variety of circumstances. They consequently are open to new interpretation and fresh application. And because of the adaptability of these proverbs, though they come to us from a civilization thousands of years old, they speak to us with truth and freshness, and they hit home even today.

An Introduction to the Proverbs (1:1–7)

The opening words of our scripture lesson give us the title: "The proverbs of Solomon the son of David, king of Israel" (1:1, KJV). Bible students over the years have discussed whether this is to be taken as a general title for the whole book or only for the first nine chapters. It is, of course, possible that originally it stood as a heading only for the smaller collection and then later was taken as a general title.

The word for proverb in the Hebrew language is *māshāl,* which means "that which represents or signifies" something. A proverb is a saying, a parable, a statement, or a question that represents—re-*presents*—reality. It is a true, faithful, and wise statement. So what we have here are wise sayings that a person can rely on as guides through life, because they faithfully reflect reality.

An Introductory "Advertisement"

Books often appear—as this one does—with an introductory preface, a brief explanation of what is to follow. This is sometimes a form of advertisement, much like the descriptive and enticing text on the back cover of a paperback, that invites us into the book and promises that our time will be well spent. These first few verses of our scripture lesson—verses 2 through 7—are this kind of introductory advertisement.

First, we're told that the reason for this book is so we may "know wisdom" (1:2, ESV); to "know" wisdom is to become acquainted with right actions. The emphasis, in other words, is placed upon practical living rather than theoretical knowledge. Wisdom, for the Hebrews, was more ethics than it was philosophy. For them, a person was wise when he or she acted wisely—saving money rather than squandering it, treating a neighbor with courtesy and good judgment.

So firmly was the Hebrew mindset on the practical characteristics of wisdom that their definitions often extended to skills and abilities clearly outside what we would normally label as "wise." In Exodus 28:3, for example, the idea of wisdom refers to technical skill. In Isaiah 10:13 it is used to describe military arts. And sometimes, as in 1 Kings 2:6, it is even used to imply cleverness.

Second, we learn that we will "receive the instruction of wisdom" (1:3, KJV). Now, in a way, this sounds like the same idea expressed in verse 2. But something more is intended here. The implication is that there is a discipline or practice that will produce wisdom. We know by experience that skills are developed with practice. For example, if we want to learn to play the piano, practice is one of the most important ways in which to improve our skills. The idea expressed here is that wisdom increases with disciplined practice.

Third, we are told that we will receive instruction in justice or righteousness. This is also an area of life where we grow through disciplined practice. Then the writer goes on to promise "judgment" and "equity" (verse 3, KJV). Judgment is the quality of knowing the right thing or the just thing to do in relating to other people. It involves a sense of "equity" or fairness and impartiality.

Finally, this little introduction promises what the book will do for different kinds of people (1:4–6). It applies to the disadvantaged as well as the social elite. In other words, the treasure of proverbs is for everybody!

The Key Note
We come next to a statement that will be echoed throughout the book of Proverbs, "The fear of the Lord is the beginning of knowledge" (1:7, KJV). This is such an important idea in all of Wisdom literature that we must be very clear about what is meant by "fear." It does not refer to fear of danger or mean

that we are frightened or scared. Rather, the word *fear* as the Wisdom writer is using it means "awe" or "reverence" in the presence of God. In other words, wisdom comes from a certain attitude toward God. It comes from a recognition and an experience of who God is—and of who we are in His presence.

The writer goes on immediately to add, "but fools despise wisdom and instruction" (1:7, NIV). We shouldn't take this to mean that a person despises wisdom and instruction—discipline—because he or she is a fool. Rather, we understand that a person is a fool *because* he or she despises wisdom and instruction. Such discipline and knowledge can only be ours when we are willing to pay the price for them. And since discipline is painful, strenuous, and costly, there are many who won't get wisdom. Their failure to get wisdom, however, is not an intellectual failure; rather it is being unwilling to pay the price.

Now, if we bring these two parts of verse 7 together, we can see something extraordinarily important about the insight of the Wisdom writer. On the one hand, we see that coming before Almighty God is awe-inspiring, even fear-provoking. We find it much easier to avoid the ultimate reality of life, death, and our utter dependence upon God. Life seems more comfortable if we can drift and look the other way and ignore God. But when we are confronted by our own helplessness, we know it doesn't work. It is then we become "awestruck," "unsettled," and come to know our complete dependence upon God.

However—and this pertains to the second part of verse 7—when we willingly endure the discipline of turning to God, we have put ourselves on the path to wisdom. We may be shaken to the very root of our being, and we may be dislodged from our comfortable view of life, but this is precisely the "price" of wisdom. Those who endure "fear" will find wisdom.

This means that those life-shaping trials and hard times that we encounter have done us a great service. Through them, we have discovered God even though we may not have realized it at the time. It is in and through life's difficult moments that we learn reverence for God and begin to learn wisdom. Though we celebrate and even brag about our successes, it is often through failures and crises that we learn the important lessons of life and gain wisdom.

The Value of Learned Truth (1:8–19)

There is something irreplaceable about what we learn from our parents and teachers—the early mentors and guides who instruct and model for us how to live. Here, the Wisdom writer appeals to his reader to remember those irreplaceable truths learned from father and mother (1:8). Then in picture language, he goes on to say that parental instruction both enriches life and is a valuable inheritance (1:9).

An Important Warning

Along with this praise of instruction received from parents, the writer draws a sharp contrast as he warns his readers to resist the temptation of sin and of sinful people (1:10). The warning is clear. We are to avoid being lured into participating in acts of violence against the lives and property of others (1:11–14). Any form of false teaching that offers an easy way or a shortcut to wealth is to be avoided at all costs.

The teaching of easy wealth appeals to us with a superficial logic. But the Proverbs writer says, in effect, "Look deeper, see where this leads." And, in a compelling picture of the foolish ways of violence and intrigue, he points to the heart of the problem.

The great Greek philosopher Plato taught that a person who is unjust to others is actually harming himself more than anyone. This is precisely the point the Proverbs writer makes. When we set a trap for strangers, he says, in reality, we set a trap for ourselves.

In contrast to the beauty that comes from parents who teach wisdom (1:9), young people who pursue violence "lie in wait for their own blood" (1:18, NIV); they are on the road to self-destruction.

Wisdom's Call and Wisdom's Despisers (1:20–33)

Wisdom as a Person

Our writer now employs a literary device we call "personification"—he characterizes wisdom as a person, a woman. Here wisdom is pictured as walking in the streets and wherever people gather, calling out her message: "Out in the open wisdom calls aloud, she raises her voice in the public square; on top of the wall she cries out, at the city gate she makes her speech" (1:20–21, NIV). Today the writer might have worded it this way: "Wisdom calls out to the tourists in Times Square and the traders on Wall Street, her voice rings out in the lecture halls of Harvard and Stanford, it echoes in the boutiques of Beverly Hills and in the halls of Congress." The point is that she is heard everywhere, but at every point, she is ignored—no one pays any attention to what she says.

Wisdom Is Available to Everyone
The writer is working with two important ideas in these verses. In verses 20–23, he wants his first readers—and us—to understand that wisdom isn't some secret or hidden thing. The ways of life are open to us. A large part of wisdom is what we would often call "common sense" and is available to everyone. Some things we learn from observation. Others we get through imitation. Wisdom is passed from generation to generation through traditions and customs. In other words, wisdom is present and available wherever we are, and we could learn from it if only we would listen.

The Importance of Listening
The second idea (1:24–33) is that in spite of everything, a great many people do not listen. "Because I have called and you refused to listen, have stretched out my hand and no one has heeded . . . I also will laugh at your calamity; I will mock when terror strikes you (1:24, 26, ESV).

Now the Bible doesn't focus on the *skill* of listening, but it does call attention to something much more basic—the *intention* to listen. Giving our attention to others and to the world around us is important to our learning process.

In the story of Solomon's early reign as king of Israel, we read that he asked God to give him "an understanding heart"—wisdom (1 Kings 3:5–9 in most translations). A few

Bible versions render it in its more literal translation: "a listening heart." This gets us closer to the biblical idea of wisdom. The root of the wise life is a willingness to listen. Or, to put it another way, it is a willingness to be open and attentive to a world in which wisdom is abundantly present.

Along with this idea, we can see that the unwillingness to listen is often related to an unwillingness to be found at fault. It is related to the reluctance we all have when we are found to be wrong. At such times we would benefit greatly from admitting our fault and accepting reproof and correction. This is the point the Proverbs writer is making when he has Wisdom say, "If you turn at my reproof, behold, I will pour out my spirit to you; I will make my words known to you" (1:23, ESV).

"He who does not judge himself," says an old rabbinic proverb, "will be judged by all things, all things become messengers from God." The Wisdom writer is confident that we will all, sooner or later, learn this lesson that Wisdom has for us. The way to learn "sooner" is by listening to the lessons Wisdom teaches—in experience, by tradition, by the insights of others, and especially by the revealed truth of Scripture. But the way we learn "later," unfortunately, is often through failure, abandonment, disaster, and desolation.

The Pursuit of Wisdom Leads to God (2:1–22)

A pattern is emerging here in this opening section of the book of Proverbs: Wisdom is from God, therefore the pursuit of wisdom leads to God. This idea can also be stated in another way. When we move into the presence of God, we discover wisdom. The two ideas sound paradoxical: pursue God and we find wisdom; pursue wisdom and we find God. They are really two ways of expressing the same basic truth. First, the emphasis is on pursuing wisdom (2:2–5). Next, the emphasis is on seeking God (2:6–11).

In this part of our scripture lesson we are urged to enter into a pursuit of wisdom—and of God. Notice how the words imply an impassioned longing, yearning, searching—an impassioned pursuit. To his basic instruction, "My son, *if* you accept my words and store up my commands within you" (2:1, NIV), the writer adds, "Indeed, *if* you call out for insight and cry aloud for understanding, and *if* you look for it as for silver and search for it as for hidden treasure" (2:3–4, emphasis added). Here a condition is implied. "If . . . if . . . if. . . ." The condition of ardent pursuit and searching sets up a promise.

So, if this is the condition of the promise, what is the fulfillment? What happens when we pursue wisdom with all our heart? We get our answer in the next verses (2:5–9): (1) We shall understand the fear of God (awe, reverence of God), and, by implication, we will experience His presence (2:5); (2) we will find the knowledge and wisdom of God (2:5–6); and (3) we will understand righteousness, judgment, and equity—in other words, we'll know the right path to take (2:7–9). Notice, once again, the double promise—each reflecting the same idea. Pursue God and we find wisdom; pursue wisdom and we find God.

Some people disparage the idea of seeking after wisdom as a way to God. They feel this approach is intellectual as opposed to "spiritual." But for the Hebrew Wisdom writer this was a very important part of our seeking after God—as it was for many Christians in the Middle Ages. And in more modern times we can find well-known examples of Christian leaders whose search for God was, first of all, a search for understanding. C. S. Lewis, the Oxford and Cambridge scholar who became famous for his writings on Christianity, is a leading example. Malcolm Muggeridge, the English journalist, is another example, as is Dorothy Sayers, the famous novelist and essayist. They each found God, but the events that brought them to Him took the form of a pursuit of wisdom and understanding.

Others, however, were first struck by the powerful presence of God in life, and this experience led to a clarity of understanding they would not have known otherwise. Thomas Merton, the Trappist monk, tried at first to escape the conflicts of a sick and troubled world. But in the process of finding God, he also discovered a new understanding and awareness of the world he at first wanted to escape.

Both of these ways of discovering the truth of God recognize a common reality: The truth of God and the God of truth are inseparable ideas.

Two Ways Contrasted

As we move along in the footsteps of the Wisdom writer, we become aware of something very important about the Hebrew concept of wisdom (2:10–22). Wisdom is not simply an intellectual virtue. It is the ability to choose between certain courses of action—and the will to choose the right one. It is much more practical and much less theoretical than we often assume.

Inherent in the teaching of wisdom is the necessity of making a choice. This is often expressed as the two "ways," or the two "paths." First, there is the way of life (2:10–11). Then there is the path of darkness and death (2:12–19). The effect of wisdom is that "you will walk in the way of good people and keep to the paths of the righteous" (2:20, NASB). The ends of the two ways are life and death. "For the upright [those who are in right standing with God] will live in the land and those [of integrity] who are blameless [in God's sight] will remain in it; but the wicked will be cut off from the land and the treacherous shall be [forcibly] uprooted and removed from it" (2:21–22, AMP).

In making his point the writer draws upon an example that he will return to several times—the young man who is seduced into sexual sin. The idea of the "two ways" is vividly drawn; the contrast is stark. Wisdom is able to deliver us from sexual sin (2:16), from the way that "leads down to death. . . . None who go to her return" (2:18–19, NIV). Because the way of wisdom is "the way of good men," and "the paths of life" (3:19–20, KJV).

Throughout the book of Proverbs we will be reminded again and again of the sacredness of marriage and of the family. But the writer intends to make an even broader case against sin. In a way, marriage can become a test, and an example, of the right and wrong paths. The point being made is that all sin is like adultery, it is the breaking of a covenant. It is disloyalty to a sacred relationship between two persons.

People of ancient Israel believed that disease often follows sexual sin. They believed that even if it does not affect the body, it certainly destroys the health of the heart and mind. The Proverbs writer understood the relationship between the enticing sin and its destructive results, and he wanted to make the point that all sin, like this sin of adultery, is a one-way avenue to death.

Advice to a Son Concerning Wisdom (3:1–35)

We often hear the book of Proverbs referred to as "the young man's book." It is easy to see how this description applies, since so much of Proverbs is interlaced with earnest appeals to "my son." In this part of our scripture lesson we have three distinct poems, each addressed to "my son." The themes can be picked up by looking at the first line of each of the three: (1) "My son, do not forget my teaching" (3:1, ESV); (2) "My son, do not despise the Lord's discipline" (3:11); (3) "My son, do not lose sight of . . . sound wisdom and discretion" (3:21).

Keeping the Law

In the first poem we see that life itself—both its quality and its length—depends upon faithfulness to the law, and the heart of keeping the law is obedience to God. The writer of the book of Judges warned repeatedly of the dire consequences to a whole nation when "everyone did what was right in his own eyes" (Judges 21:25, ESV).

The biblical writer, and especially the Wisdom writer—the sage—warned against the danger of following only our own thoughts and opinions. He was highly suspicious of what we might call "radical individualism."

Wisdom—a Community Treasure

Wisdom, as the writer recognizes, is a possession of a whole community. It is passed on in traditions, so it includes a community that goes far beyond a single generation. When the commandment is given—"Honor your father and your mother"—it recognizes the fact that one generation depends upon another. The commandment continues, as you'll recall, "so that your days may be prolonged on the land which the Lord your God gives you" (Exodus 20:12, NASB). Life and community—the community of one generation following another—are tied together.

The point that wisdom depends upon community—and is not an individual possession—is not so much *taught* by the book of Proverbs as it is *assumed*. We see that wisdom comes from a deeper source than the understanding provided by an individual life: "Trust in the Lord with all your heart and lean not [do not depend] on your own understanding" (3:5, NIV). Instead, "in all your ways submit to him, and he will make your paths straight" (3:6, NIV).

The Discipline of Difficulty

In the second poem (3:11–20), the young man is told, "Do not reject the discipline of the Lord" (NASB). We often learn our most valuable lessons in life through pain and trouble—even the hard times we bring on ourselves by our own mistakes. "Good judgment comes from experience," goes an old adage, "and experience comes from bad judgment." The discipline of difficulty can become the surest route to wisdom.

When we say that difficulty can become the route to wisdom, we are recognizing that another condition must also be present. It is possible for difficulty to lead to bitterness, frustration, and fear. We can close ourselves off from life and resent our circumstances. The third poem in this series (3:21–35) urges us to face circumstances with faith. Faith, as the German theologian Jürgen Moltmann has often said, is not the opposite of doubt, but it is the opposite of fear. The Proverbs writer speaks of facing life with faith in these words: "If you lie down, you will not be afraid; when you lie down, your sleep will be sweet. Do not be afraid of sudden terror or of the ruin of the wicked, when it comes, for the Lord will be your confidence and will keep your foot from being caught" (3:24–26, ESV).

If we reflect carefully on our own habits, or on the habitual attitudes of others, we will come to recognize that much personal suffering comes as a result of unjust action. In his great dialogue, *The Republic,* Plato makes the point that the person who is happiest is also one who is fairest and most just in his or her dealings with others. It is not a coincidence that the proverbs that call for wisdom as an antidote to fear are followed by brief sentences that urge living a just and upright life: Do good when you can (3:27); give each what is due (3:28); don't delay in paying your debts (3:28); don't plot against your neighbor (3:29); don't engage in strife (3:30), nor envy those who oppress (3:31)—for wisdom and justice bring security and blessings.

Wisdom Is the Fullest Understanding of Life (4:1–27)

Madeleine L'Engle's book *The Summer of the Great-Grandmother* is about the last year of her mother's life. Her mother's approaching death caused the author to reflect on the heritage of stories and experiences that had been passed on to her through her mother. Throughout the book she recounts the family traditions of her parents, grandparents, and great-grandparents. Many of us have a rich inheritance in the words and actions of those who have gone before us. This is a sobering thought when we realize that our children and grandchildren will look to us for wisdom and direction in the shaping of their lives.

The first few verses of this part of our scripture lesson make up an ode to the great worth of a father's wisdom (4:1–4). Here the writer pays tribute to "a father's instruction" (verse 1, ESV) that sets a good and noble example: "he taught me and said to me, 'Let your heart hold fast my words; keep my commandments, and live'" (verse 4).

This part of our lesson brings to us an awareness of three vital principles. *First*, it is important for us to pass on the experiences and lessons of wisdom from one generation to another. The familiar adage "Those who do not learn the lessons of history are condemned to repeat them" applies here. This is a responsibility that rests primarily with the older generation: to reflect seriously upon their own experience, to know what God has taught them through these experiences, and to pass on those truths to their children and grandchildren. The Wisdom writer said, "For I give you good teaching; do not abandon my instruction" (4:2, NASB), and he remembered how his own father taught him (4:4).

Second, it is the responsibility of the younger generation to listen and to actively pursue, cherish, and keep that which has been passed on (4:1, 5, 6, 8, and 13).

Third, the primary place where the transfer of wisdom from one generation to another is accomplished is, of course, in the home. The book of Proverbs speaks vividly and forcefully to family life. It is concerned with fathers and mothers and children—because it is within the family that instruction in wisdom can most effectively take place.

The Importance of Sexual Discipline (5:1–23)

Continuing to speak as the father or teacher, the writer urges "my son" to avoid any form of sexual sin and involvement with "a forbidden woman" (Proverbs 5:3, ESV). As we read this part of our scripture lesson, several things must be kept in mind.

1. The warning here is directed toward men, and the subject is the adulterous and seductive woman whose smooth talk could lure a virile young man into sexual indiscretions. However, in our twenty-first-century society these same warnings apply just as readily to young women.
2. Sexuality itself is never condemned. The suspicion with which the very fact of sexuality is treated by many ancient moralists is never found among the Hebrew Wisdom writers. Just the

opposite is the case. Sexuality is a part of the good things in life given by a loving God who affirms human relationships in general and sexual relations in particular. It is part of what God labeled as "very good" at the time of creation.

3. Adultery and sexual indiscretions of any kind lead to a host of disastrous consequences: (a) loss of honor (5:9); (b) dissipation of life and effort that should be spent in a more profitable way (5:10); (c) disease and death (5:11). These same consequences are just as much with us today as they were with our spiritual ancestors in Israel three thousand years ago, and they give ample reason for wisdom, honesty, and restraint in sexual conduct.

4. Married sex offers great rewards: (a) growing and continuing affection is experienced by the loving married couple (5:15–18); (b) pleasure (5:19) is not disparaged but is a strong argument for fidelity in marriage; and (c) a life honored by God (5:21) is promised when we are wise in our sexual conduct.

Certainly, our twenty-first-century culture is drastically different from that of the people of Israel over three thousand years ago. But human nature has changed little, if at all. Faithfulness in marriage and family is still the glue that holds everything of value together.

A Life Well Invested (6:1–19)

At first glance it would seem that the book of Proverbs is little more than a collection of warnings—watch out for this . . . be careful for that! It is true, of course, that many of the warnings

are directed against very common everyday problems. In verses 1–19, for instance, the sayings elaborate on three basic principles of life:
1. Don't be a guarantor (put up security) for another person's debt (6:1–5);
2. Be industrious, not lazy (6:6–11); and
3. Be honest, not deceitfully clever (6:12–15).

All of these hold up the ideal of an open, honest, and well-ordered life. A reward is assured for those who invest their time well, guard the integrity of their word, and tell the truth.

A Model of Self-Discipline

In this part of our lesson the Wisdom writer chose a familiar symbol of self-discipline and hard work as he wrote, "Go to the ant, O sluggard; consider her ways, and be wise" (6:6, ESV). Here we have a model of the wise person who is industrious and plans carefully.

Then this part of our scripture lesson closes with a dire warning against seven sins that constitute antisocial behavior: a proud look, lying, murder, a conniving mind, a determination to exercise self-will, bearing false witness against another person, and being a troublemaker (6:16–19). It's amazing, isn't it? You'd think someone was giving a sort of reverse TED Talk on how not to make friends and influence people!

The Perils of Illicit Sex (6:20–7:27)

We have already seen that the single most frequent warning we find in the book of Proverbs is against adultery and illicit sexual relations. In this part of our lesson we find a vivid description of the strength and power of sexual temptation. Without a doubt, these inviting and seductive words credited to an adulterous woman who looks like a prostitute are persuasive: "Come, let's drink our fill of love until morning; let's delight ourselves with caresses. For my husband is not at home; he has gone on a long journey" (7:18–19, NASB).

Earlier, though, the Wisdom writer spells out in graphic detail the dreadful consequences of giving in to illicit and adulterous sex: "Another man's wife preys on your very life" (6:26, NIV). "But a man who commits adultery has no sense; whoever does so destroys himself" (6:32, NIV). "All at once he followed her like an ox going to the slaughter, like a deer stepping into a noose till an arrow pierces his liver, like a bird darting into a snare, little knowing it will cost him his life " (7:22–23, NIV). "Her house is a highway to the grave, leading down to the chambers of death" (7:27, NIV).

The writer of the book of Proverbs draws the picture so that we see clearly how sexual conduct is related to all of life. Television series, movies, the internet, all of them try to seduce us into thinking that illicit sex is an acceptable way of life. But intuitively we know this isn't true, even in today's world.

The Personification of Wisdom

The personification of Wisdom is a striking feature of the book of Proverbs. At several points "she" appears: 1:20–33; 3:13–18; 8:1–21; 8:22–31; 9:1–6. In contrast to the adulterous woman described in chapter 7, who was guilty of whispering enticing words in secret, this Wisdom figure speaks openly, in public, to everyone. She speaks forthrightly of the virtues of honesty (8:6–7) and prudence (8:12). She praises the gift of insight and understanding (8:14), and she herself lives a righteous and just life (8:20).

When the writer says that this person of Wisdom was created at the very beginning of all things and was involved in the creative process (8:22–31), he is relating wisdom to the very nature of God. With superb skill the poet employs the strongest possible figures of speech to show that wisdom, prudence, honor, goodness, and justice are the attributes of God.

Then in the closing verses of chapter 8 the Wisdom person urges her listeners to pay careful attention to her words and pursue her way of life. A blessing is given to those who do— and a promise: "Blessed is the one who listens to me. . . . For whoever finds me finds life and obtains favor from the Lord" (8:34–35, ESV).

Wisdom Versus Foolishness

Now, as the writer moves toward the close of this part of the book of Proverbs, we are treated to a study in contrasts (9:1–18). First we have a scene that is reminiscent of Jesus's parable of the marriage supper (Matthew 22:1–14). Like the king in Jesus's story, Wisdom issues an invitation for everyone to accept her hospitality: "Come, eat my food and drink the wine I have mixed [and accept my gifts]. Leave [behind] your foolishness [and the foolish] and live, and walk in the way of insight and understanding" (9:5–6, AMP).

Next follow several wisdom sayings, and among them is one that sets the mood for the entire book of Proverbs: "The fear of the Lord is the beginning of wisdom: and the knowledge of the holy is understanding" (9:10, KJV). Since the day the writer wrote those words our world has undergone drastic changes. But even in our age of space travel, smartphones, and robotic surgery, these words apply to us just as much, if not more, than they did to their first readers.

Finally, in vivid contrast to the personification of wisdom, the writer gives us the personification of foolishness. As Foolishness issues her invitation for people to follow her, she is noisy and shameless (9:13). She flaunts her wiles to the "simple" and uses a proverb associated with illicit sex: "Stolen waters are sweet, and bread eaten in secret is pleasant" (9:17, KJV). Her seductive appeal may be strong, but her guests are already in the place of death (9:18).

Summary

The images used throughout this scripture lesson are powerful and have been offered with great literary skill. They are, of course, quite different in form from much of our thinking and way of life. There is a wide gap between their ancient Near East setting and our pragmatic Western ways. Yet the truths so colorfully presented are up-to-date and relevant to our time.

- Authentic life-giving and life-preserving wisdom and insight can only be found in our awe and reverence for God. It gives life in our complex modern world a satisfaction and meaning that cannot be found elsewhere.

- A style of life that ignores wisdom may appear at times to be seductively attractive and exciting, but its appeal is short-lived because it leads to darkness, self-deception, and death.
- To pursue wisdom as a way of life is to pursue God Himself—the Source of life.

Lord, lead us in the paths of wisdom and in the ways of a full and purposeful life. Save us from our self-imposed foolishness so that we can serve You with a pure heart and clear vision. AMEN.

Happy is the man that findeth wisdom.

—Proverbs 3:13 (KJV)

"Hey, Brock, look what I found in my desk drawer," my mother says, handing me an envelope. It is made of a fine paper that texting and emails have pretty much made extinct. The handwriting is old-school beautiful. "Mr. Brockwell Kidd" is written there. I touch the embossed name on the back flap, Madison S. Wigginton.

   I suppose I was a pushy kid when I decided, about halfway through high school, that I needed a mentor and chose Mr. Wigginton. Maybe being a preacher's kid like me caused him to say yes. Whatever his thinking, he granted me an appointment.

   Mr. Wigginton was, before he retired, one of Nashville's preeminent businessmen. He lived in an elegant house in a posh neighborhood, widowed and alone. The first time I knocked on his door, a butler answered. "Mr. Kidd?" he asked. I stopped myself from turning around to see if my dad was standing behind me. I sat in a wingback chair, drinking tea, munching on a macaroon, waiting for Mr. Wigginton to appear. He was around ninety, tall, and spry. His voice was deep, and his eyes told me his heart was young.

  I asked for advice. He talked of the importance of friendship and of loyalty to others in business. And so our visits went, sound advice offered to an eager kid. The last time I saw Mr. Wigginton, he was standing on the sideline of the football field at my high-school graduation. Earlier, we had enjoyed one last visit. His parting advice: "Love people and try to understand them." I carry his words with me even now.

Father, You send messengers to impart Your wisdom. Help us to be wise enough to listen.

—*Brock Kidd*

The earliest recorded wisdom writings appeared in the ancient Near East before the time of Abraham in Mesopotamia. Proverbs and other forms of wisdom writing surfaced in Egypt around 2500 BC. With Egypt's sophisticated culture it isn't at all surprising that it became a repository for the thinking of their sages, including their famed but ill-fated Library of Alexandria. One way or another Egyptian influence hovered over the people of Israel throughout all of Bible times.

Another contributor to wisdom thinking in ancient times was the rather unlikely country of Edom, not far from the famous city of Petra. In 1 Kings 4:30–31 the "sons of Mahol" were wise men of Edom, and the wisdom of Edom is mentioned briefly by the prophet Jeremiah (49:7). The rugged country of both Edom and Arabia was apparently congenial to wisdom thinking.

As we have seen, the wisdom literature in the Bible had its beginnings around 1000 BC and is closely associated with Solomon, the king of Israel during its golden age.

It was Solomon who enlarged Jerusalem and who built the temple for worship of the Lord God. The glory of Solomon's Jerusalem was known throughout the ancient Near East, as was his reputation for being a wise man: "And Solomon's wisdom excelled the wisdom of all the children of the east country, and all the wisdom of Egypt" (1 Kings 4:30, KJV).

It was to Jerusalem that the Queen of Sheba came in search of the truth about Solomon's wisdom and the beauty of the city. When she had listened to Solomon and seen the city, she said, "The report was true that I heard in my own land of your words and of your wisdom, but I did not believe the reports until I came and my own eyes had seen it. And behold, the half was not told me. Your wisdom and prosperity surpass the report that I heard" (1 Kings 10:6–7, ESV).

Notes

Notes

Notes

LESSON 2: PROVERBS 10:1–22:16

The Two Ways: Wisdom Contrasted with Folly

Lord, grant me wisdom—especially the wisdom to discern what is wise and what is foolish. Amen.

We all learn by comparing new experiences or ideas with what we already know. An unfamiliar concept may seem just out of reach. We would say it is "over our heads." But an apt comparison between the unfamiliar and the familiar helps us to understand better. A good teacher uses comparisons to make the strange and foreign more familiar, to bring the difficult within easy range, or to scale down complexities.

This ability to teach by comparison is the great strength of the book of Proverbs. These ancient Hebrew verses are made up of observations about the things people see and feel and think about every day. They become stepladders to the teaching of great truths about living, using common experiences to teach us uncommon wisdom.

Some of the examples and comparisons from ancient life may seem foreign to us. But it is remarkable that most of them have an up-to-date sound. Fathers still give advice to sons; diligence and indolence are qualities that concern us today as they did the ancients; people still make money, save it, lend it, waste it, and lose it. Discretion, prudence, judgment, honesty, truth, faithfulness—these concerns will not be foreign to us, for the issues are basic to our human condition.

Time has changed the language and colored the attitudes, but the issues themselves enable us to reach out and link hands with endless generations through history.

Simple Yet Profound

One of the utterly delightful things about the book of Proverbs is the way in which the writer puts profound truth into the simplest terms. The language is plain and to the point. It is direct, though at first the ideas discussed might seem to be expressed in terms that are too broad. The reservations are missing. The subtleties of real life are left out.

But we need to remember that Proverbs is a book of lessons, a teaching book. It is lessons passed on from parent to child or from teacher to student.

When we understand Proverbs in this light, it is not difficult to see that there is a necessity for first lessons as well as advanced lessons. No professor in graduate school could do his work well if, somewhere along the line, someone had not taught reading, writing, and arithmetic at the elementary level. The fact that a lesson is simple and elementary does not disprove its value.

So let's look at these writings as a primer in moral teachings—a collection of first lessons that outline the broad truths. For example, in broad strokes the Wisdom writer insists that the righteous shall prosper. Now, we know that the righteous do not *always* prosper, certainly not in a material sense. And in less than a minute you can probably think of five exceptions to that rule.

Such exceptions are highlighted in other parts of Scripture. This is vividly illustrated in the books of Job and Habakkuk. Then, as we'll see later in this volume, the writer of Ecclesiastes wonders about the ultimate value of hard work, learning, and prosperity.

But these exceptions tend only to reinforce the rule. In spite of the seeming contradictions, we also know there is a basic and elementary lesson to be learned. We know that where there is no prudence, wisdom, patience, diligence, honesty, and charity, there will also be no prosperity. That is the *first* lesson. It doesn't cover everything, but it does lay the foundation.

And that is what these proverbs do—they provide the first lesson. The book of Proverbs is our primer for the moral concepts of the Old Testament. And we need to be reminded of this fact before we can fully appreciate the more advanced lessons of Old Testament moral thinking.

The Proverbs of Solomon (10:1)

"The Proverbs of Solomon" is the original title of the scripture that makes up our entire lesson (10:1–22:16). It is generally believed to be the oldest section of the book of Proverbs and probably was written during the reign of King Solomon over Israel, 961–922 BC. Most certainly, Solomon was known for his wisdom, a reputation that comes from the account of his early reign in 1 Kings 3 and 4. And these proverbs are the greatest monument that we have to Solomon's God-given wisdom.

Notice that two sections of the book of Proverbs are headed with a title that attributes them to Solomon. Besides this section (10:1–22:16), there is the section between 25:1 and 29:27 that is given a similar title. If we were looking for a core to the book, these two sections could well be considered the heart of the entire collection. Here we find the major themes and the typical attitudes and values of Israel's sages.

As we read this section, we notice that it is made up almost entirely of thoughts presented in two phrases, the second reinforcing the idea of the first. Sometimes the second phrase repeats in different words the thought of the first phrase, as in 11:25: "A generous person will be prosperous, and one who gives others plenty of water will himself be given plenty" (NASB).

At other times the first phrase states a truth and the second presents its opposite. For example, "When the tempest passes, the wicked is no more, but the righteous is established forever" (10:25, ESV). This type is called an antithetical statement.

Most of the proverbs in chapters 10 through 15 are very effective antithetical statements. They are effective for three reasons:

1. They are brief statements, capturing an idea in a few words, making it easy to remember.
2. Stating the idea first one way and then the other is an important rhetorical device. It gives the impression of finality and authority. In effect, it "opens" the subject and "closes" it. "This is true," it says, "but this is not." The subject is fenced in by the two approaches in the two brief phrases.
3. The antithetical phrasing and the short, direct statements bear the beauty of simplicity, and with simplicity comes strength.

The Rewards of Righteous Living (10:2–12:28)

The Disciplined Life

In this part of our scripture lesson the Wisdom writer brings a few themes to our attention again and again. Notice, for instance, how frequently the disciplined life is mentioned. The writer sees it as an aspect of the righteous life. Diligence, hard work, and a vigorous life produce great rewards and are thoroughly praised.

"Lazy hands make for poverty," says the writer, "but diligent hands bring wealth" (10:4, NIV). In other words, the making of wealth comes from a willingness to pay the price with discipline and vigor. The expression "No pain, no gain!" is popular among athletes, who know that improving their performance results only from the hard work of physical training. This is a modern expression of precisely the Wisdom writer's point of view. Every reward has its price. If we avoid the price, through laziness and slackness, we cannot expect to gain wealth or anything of value.

According to the Wisdom writer, another feature of the disciplined life is a willingness to be taught. One of the great assets that is needed for any progress in life is a teachable attitude. Pride prevents this willingness to be taught and to receive instruction. Humility, on the other hand, is more than anything else a teachable heart: "The wise of heart will receive commandments, but a babbling fool will come to ruin" (10:8, ESV). A person who truly hopes to gain knowledge and wisdom "loves discipline," while "the one who hates rebuke is stupid" (12:1, NASB).

The Rewards of Humility

There is an irony in this last saying. If we are humble and willing to think that we are still ignorant enough to be taught, we shall gain real knowledge. But if we are proud and think too highly of ourselves so that we cannot be taught, we will be less human—more "stupid" as several translations word it.

The Old Testament revels in this particular truth. It is David, the unlikeliest son of Jesse, who becomes king, while Saul in his presumptuous pride loses his kingdom. It is those enslaved in Egypt who receive God's message, not the pharoah. It is those who are deported to Babylon in the Captivity who, later, carry on the traditions and the glory of Israel, not those "fortunate" ones who are left behind. The high are made low, but the low are lifted up. "When pride comes, then comes disgrace, but with the humble is wisdom" (11:2, ESV).

Material Wealth

Material wealth is also a major focus in this part of our lesson. The Proverbs writer teaches on the one hand that wealth is a blessing received with thanksgiving by those who live uprightly: "The Lord will not suffer the soul of the righteous to famish . . . . the hand of the diligent maketh rich" (10:3–4, KJV). "The rich man's wealth is his strong city" (10:15, KJV).

But, on the other hand, those who live sinful and dishonest lives are headed for ruin. "The hope of the righteous brings joy, but the expectation of the wicked will perish" (10:28, ESV). "When a wicked person dies, his expectation will perish, and the hope of strong people perishes" (11:7, NASB).

When Good Is Given, Good Is Returned
Another idea is prominent in this section: When good is given, good is returned. There is a paradox in that idea—a person who gives freely has no needs, but a person who selfishly holds on to things suffers want. The Bible is full of instructions to be generous, often accompanied by promises of God's generosity when we give freely. Paul quoted Jesus in Acts 20:35: "He Himself said, 'It is more blessed to give than to receive'" (NASB). Jesus might well have had this proverb in mind when He said this: "A generous person will prosper; whoever refreshes others will be refreshed" (11:25, NIV).

Outward Appearance Can Be Deceptive
The outward appearance of things is often deceptive. The writer of Proverbs was well aware of this and took many opportunities in this section to drive home the point. Beauty does not tell the full story, for "like a gold ring in a pig's snout is a beautiful woman who shows no discretion" (11:22, NIV).

Wealth Is No Insurance against Trouble
An aspect of the deceptiveness of appearances is seen in the fact that wealth can come to those who are undeserving and without honor: "[R]uthless men gain only wealth" (11:16, NIV), and the Amplified Bible qualifies it: "Ruthless men attain riches [but not respect]." The writer also tells us that the "wicked earns deceptive wages, but one who sows righteousness gets a sure reward" (11:18, ESV). But that isn't the whole story. The acquiring of wealth is no insurance

against trouble, but righteousness and honesty provide strength to overcome trouble (11:4–5).

We might well ask, "What are those troubles for which obedience to God and not wealth give an answer?" The Wisdom writer provides us with some answers in chapter 11. We will look briefly at the following: (1) death (11:4); (2) the need for guidance (11:5); (3) evil (11:6); (4) futile expectations (11:7).

Death

First, let's look at what could be called the ultimate evil—death. We're all familiar with the saying "You can't take it with you." Much humor, as well as serious reflection, has been spent on this truth. Let's face it, wealth is good only while our health is good and we're alive. When illness and age come and death becomes a real prospect, we see the true limitation and the ultimate uselessness of money and material possessions.

But next it is logical for us to ask just why obedience to God—righteousness—provides an answer to the perplexing anxiety about death. In response we can say that righteousness means that life, even within its earthly and mortal limits, has been lived well. It means that our life has served a good cause and purpose and can be looked back upon with satisfaction. There is just no way that wealth and material possessions can give us peace of mind and the satisfying feeling that our lives count and are acceptable to God. But of supreme importance to us is that in living a righteous and obedient life, we have the assurance of life beyond death and the grave.

The Need for Guidance

When we turn to the need for guidance alluded to in Proverbs 11:5, we see that righteousness is associated with an honest evaluation of ourselves and others. It is based upon and promotes clear thinking. The wisdom to do what is best and to take the right course of action, the writer saw, is secured by honest and clear thinking. Transgressors of the law, on the other hand, deal in deceit and lies—the basis of all sin. The Proverbs writer put it this way: "The thoughts of the righteous are right: but the counsels [advice] of the wicked are deceit [deceitful]" (12:5, KJV). And in truth, since people who are sold out to evil thinking and actions try to deceive others, they are, in the process, really deceiving themselves as well. Sir Walter Scott echoed this proverb when he wrote, "Oh what a tangled web we weave/When first we practice to deceive." People who live deceitful lives create a confusing network of falsehood in their world in order to gain personal advantage, and as a result, they get lost in their own maze.

Evil

In addition, the Proverbs writer considered the advantages of morally upright living when we confront adversity. In the day of trouble "the righteousness of the blameless makes their paths straight" (11:5, NIV). In contrast, "the treacherous will be caught by their own greed" (verse 6, NASB). Someone may have become rich, the writer assumes, through unprincipled cleverness and deceit. But when trouble comes, and major crises shake the very foundations of life, then the puny skills of intrigue, deceit, and thievery are of no help at all. Good character and reliable moral judgment give us strength to face the real storms of life.

Futile Expectations

"When a wicked person dies," says the Wisdom writer, "his expectation will perish, and the hope of strong people perishes" (11:7, NASB). Here, the writer is simply affirming the truth that our hope must reside in those things that survive our own death. Wicked people care for things that never last beyond their frail, mortal existence.

There is no clear teaching on life after death in the Old Testament. A few allusions to the resurrection are to be found in certain of the psalms (for instance, Psalm 49:14 and following, and 73:23–26), as well as in Isaiah (26:19) and in Job (19:25–27). But in other places the writers appear very skeptical, as in Ecclesiastes 2:15–16 where the implication is that there is no hope outside of this life. Bible scholars have noted that the idea of life after death did not become firmly rooted in Judaism until two hundred years before Christ. But, of course, this truth is vigorously taught in the New Testament. However, the belief that some things are of such lasting value that they transcend death is fully supported throughout the Old Testament.

So we see in all of this the wisdom and strength of living a righteous and obedient life. While wealth and material possessions are for the purpose of serving our needs in this life, they do not endure. On the other hand, righteous living is based upon values that last. It can be said that education is learning to distinguish that which lasts from that which does not. The Proverbs writer would agree with that idea. For him, training in righteousness is learning to live for that which lasts forever.

Other Forms of Evil

Other forms of evil besides greed are captured in the list of proverbs we find in this part of our lesson. It is made clear that people who create discord and disharmony actually end up hurting themselves far more than others. We're told that "talebearers"—gossips or slanderers—are to be censored (11:13, KJV), as are those who are cruel and unkind (11:17). And in 11:18 the Proverbs writer insists that people get what they deserve—an evil person earns deceitful or deceptive wages while an honest and upright person is properly rewarded. Lifting this whole idea into the Christian context, the Apostle Paul in writing to the churches in Galatia said, "Do not be deceived: God is not mocked, for whatever one sows, that will he also reap" (Galatians 6:7, ESV).

The Benefits of Generosity

Next comes a group of maxims about the benefits of being generous (11:24–28). We see here that the person who gives generously has sufficient possessions for his own needs, and a person who is helpful to others receives help. And finally, the point is made that a person who places confidence in or gains satisfaction out of acquiring wealth and material goods is doomed to failure and disappointment: "The righteous will thrive like a green leaf" (11:28, NIV).

We Receive What We Give

Then, as if to make absolutely certain his reader has gotten an earlier message, the Wisdom writer returns briefly to the theme that as we give, we receive. "One who diligently seeks good seeks favor, but one who seeks evil, evil will come to him" (11:27, NASB). And "whoever brings ruin on their family will inherit only wind, and the fool will be servant to the wise" (11:29, NIV).

Truth Will Prevail

Running like a thread throughout all of the book of Proverbs is the assurance that truth will always triumph and falsehood is the root of all evil. And it is this same contrast between the actions of righteous people and wicked or evil people that runs through all of chapter 12. Here, one after another, are two-line maxims that emphasize this contrast. For the most part the meaning is sufficiently clear so that we won't attempt to explain them one by one. I urge you, though, to read them thoughtfully. Then chapter 12 closes with an emphasis once again on the theme of the book—that being righteous and obedient to God is the way to life. The wording of 12:28 in the Hebrew is unclear, but most versions render it much as it is translated in the English Standard Version (ESV): "In the path of righteousness is life, and in its pathway there is no death."

Training for Wisdom (13:1–16:33)

In other kinds of literature—an essay, for example—the thought behind the writing is carried forward progressively, with each point building on what has gone before. The premise centers on a common theme or central argument. But this is not the case with the book of Proverbs.

Here, especially in the antithetical phrases from chapters 10 through 22, we have a staggering flood of wisdom. We see the same point made in so many different ways and in various forms, evoking distinct thoughts, that it can be overwhelming.

For example, take the theme of wisdom and righteousness producing life, whereas wickedness leads to death. We've run into this before, but notice now the force with which it is carried forward: "From the fruit of his mouth a man eats what is good, but the desire of the treacherous is for violence. Whoever guards his mouth preserves his life; he who opens wide his lips comes to ruin" (13:2–3, ESV). The idea being expressed here is that obedient people will be rewarded for what they say, but a rash and evil person will be ruined and destroyed.

But then the progression continues: "Righteousness guards the one whose way is blameless, but wickedness brings the sinner to ruin" (13:6, NASB). "Trouble pursues the sinner, but the righteous are rewarded with good things" (13:21, NIV). And "The fear of the Lord is a fountain of life, that one may turn away from the snares of death" (14:27, ESV).

As we read through these chapters, we find other themes that are closely related and developed in the same way. The presentation of these themes in such pithy fashion makes them irresistible. Note the example of people who are devious and false contrasted with people who are open and truthful in

Proverbs 13:5; 14:3, 5, 7, 25; 16:11. Or note the maxims on pride versus humility: 13:7, 10; 14:26; 15:1, 12, 25, 33; 16:5, 18–19.

Much of the instruction in this part of our lesson leads us to a discipline or a restraint or a specific action. This whole section involves training in wisdom. For example, there are several references to the problem of anger. How are we to respond? Remember, the writer says, "A quick-tempered person does foolish things, and the one who devises evil schemes is hated" (14:17, NIV).

The reader is also given further training in the wisdom of restraint and prudence: "One who is slow to anger has great understanding; but one who is quick-tempered exalts foolishness" (14:29, NASB). Then it follows that, as we heed this kind of advice, we are trained to speak carefully and infrequently, and when we do speak, we do so with discretion and kindness. This lesson is expressed in various forms, but none more colorful and memorable than "gracious words are a honeycomb, sweet to the soul and healing to the bones" (16:24, NIV).

Measured Observations

Not all of the proverbs or maxims in this part of our lesson teach a moral lesson or advise wise action. A few proverbs, in fact, seem only to make an observation on something that may or may not have moral implications. Examples of this include, "Where there are no oxen, the manger is clean, but much revenue [because of good crops] comes by the strength of the ox" (14:4, AMP). Or, "A person finds joy in giving an apt reply—and how good is a timely word!" (15:23, NIV).

While most of the proverbs call for some action or a specific attitude or a change of habit, these aren't so different in form from those that don't. The important thing to remember is that the strength of the book of Proverbs is in its clear perception and common sense. The point being made over and over again is that a well-ordered life is built upon wise and honest observations of things as they are.

Poverty and Riches

In reading the book of Proverbs we become acutely aware that a great deal of thought revolves around the blessings of wealth in contrast to the disadvantages of poverty. These kinds of comments appear frequently in this part of our lesson: "The poor are shunned even by their neighbors, but the rich have many friends" (14:20, NIV). We can't help but contrast this with what Jesus said in Luke 14:12–14.

Wealth, as the ancient sages saw it, came from diligence, uprightness, foresight, and wise dealing. "In all toil there is profit" (14:23, ESV), says the writer. But for those who are lazy and who lie in order to secure what is not theirs, the payoff is quite different: "but mere talk tends only to poverty" (14:23, ESV). Again, "The house of the righteous contains great treasure, but the income of the wicked brings ruin" (15:6, NIV).

At the same time, the Wisdom writer insists that wealth cannot be an end in itself. Other considerations are more important. While wisdom usually brings material gain, whereas foolishness and evil bring poverty, the true aim of every person must be wisdom, not wealth. This is graphically illustrated by the writer as he says, "Better is a little with the fear of the Lord than great treasure, and turmoil with the treasure" (15:16, NASB).

And to illustrate the idea that poverty can mean simplicity and peace, not just the squalor of a foolish and disordered life, we're told, "Better is a portion of vegetables where there is love, than a fattened ox served with hatred" (15:17, NASB).

Material gain sought as an end in itself brings on a host of problems. And when a person's goal is, mistakenly, monetary profit, the result is tragic, for "he who profits unlawfully brings suffering to his own house, but he who hates bribes [and does not receive nor pay them] will live" (15:27, AMP).

The Higher Calling (16:1–22:16)

The collection of proverbs we are studying—chapters 10 through 22:26—are specifically labeled "the proverbs of Solomon" (10:1). Each proverb in this collection has a similar structure; it consists of two statements, the second building upon what is said in the first.

As we have seen, the proverbs included in chapters 10 through 15 consist mostly of antithetical statements, meaning that the verse states a principle positively and then reiterates it negatively, or vice versa. For example, "Lying lips are an abomination to the Lord: but they that deal truly are his delight" (12:22, KJV). The verse hinges on the word "but."

With chapter 16, however, a change takes place. The proverbs in chapters 16 through 22:16 are primarily statements that build from a first expression of a principle to a positive restatement of the same principle. The second statement emphasizes or echoes the first rather than contrasting the first.

The overall pattern might be thought of in these terms:
- Chapters 10–15 A *but* B
- Chapters 16–22:16 A *and* A[1]

Notice now how the typical pattern appears in chapters 16 through 22:16: "One who pays attention to the word will find good, and blessed is one who trusts in the Lord" (16:20, NASB). "Children's children [grandchildren] are a crown to the aged, and parents are the pride of their children" (17:6, NIV).

There is a basic principle of rhetoric involved in the way these verses are framed. We get the sense that the speaker or writer is so convinced of the truth of his statement that he can easily expand upon it. Truth builds upon truth. Certainty echoes certainty. Strength reinforces strength.

Attitudes toward Poverty and Wealth

A theme that recurs frequently in this section of the book of Proverbs is one of affirming a right attitude toward poverty. We might look at this in two ways: first, the prescription for a healthy attitude toward wealth and poverty as a condition of life; second, a compassionate attitude toward the poor.

The Wisdom writer insists that there are values that exceed riches. Wealth is, generally speaking, a sign of God's favor, but most certainly it is not the greatest treasure He can bestow: "A good name is to be chosen rather than great riches, and favor is better than silver or gold" (22:1, ESV). On the other hand, some conditions—even with riches—prove the worthlessness of wealth as an end in itself: "Better a dry crust with peace and quiet than a house full of feasting, with strife" (17:1, NIV).

The surest indication that wealth and poverty are not to be taken at face value are the warnings against mistreatment of the poor. There is, for instance, the way in which God Himself identifies with the poor: "Whoever is generous to the poor lends to the Lord, and he will repay him for his deed" (19:17, ESV). But a little later the Proverbs writer says, "Whoever closes his ear to [shuts out] the cry of the poor will himself call out and not be answered" (21:13, ESV).

Poverty has always been a part of the human condition. The scenes of poverty are everywhere—on the city streets, in the outskirts of small towns, in the shanties and shacks of the countryside.

In the modern Western world, poverty is often kept out of sight and out of mind. For Jerusalem—and all of Palestine—in Bible times there was no hiding the fact that the poor lived right alongside the wealthy. City streets thronged with the poor. People begged near the busy city gates. The lame and the blind lay about in public places. Orphans ran about the Temple precincts begging for alms.

In Bible times—and in some developing countries today—the distinction between rich and poor was clear. For this reason, it is important for us even today to listen carefully to what the book of Proverbs says about the poor. Put simply it is this: The poor are God's beloved children, no less than the rich. The Proverbs writer put it this way, "The rich and the poor have a common bond, the Lord is the Maker of them all" (22:2, NASB).

That was a revolutionary idea then, and it still creates its little revolutions in human hearts. God makes no distinction between the wealthy and those who are poor. All share equally in His concern. Rich and poor share alike in the justice and grace of the Lord.

A Test of True Faith

It has been rightly said that treatment of the poor is the acid test of true religion. This certainly comes through clearly in our present lesson and throughout the entire book of Proverbs. Our writer underscored this truth in two ways. First, God makes a special promise to those who treat the poor with kindness and compassion (19:17).

Second, our writer issued a dire warning against mistreating the poor: "One who oppresses the poor to increase his wealth and one who gives gifts to the rich—both come to poverty" (22:16, NIV).

Jesus's Emphasis on Care for the Poor

Jesus emphasized the importance of our attention to the poor and less fortunate. On one occasion Jesus told a rich young man who asked, "What shall I do to inherit eternal life?" to sell everything he had "*and distribute unto the poor*" (Luke 18:18, 22, KJV, emphasis added). When Zacchaeus climbed down from the sycamore tree and met Jesus on Jericho's main street, he was transformed—his pocketbook got converted. "'Look, Lord!'" he said. "'Here and now I give half of my possessions to the poor'" (Luke 19:8, NIV). This same sensitivity to the needs of the poor and less fortunate is woven throughout the pages of our New Testament. Paul was continually taking up a collection for the poor in Jerusalem from the churches in Asia and Europe—and they gave generously (see 2 Corinthians 8–9).

Our Responsibility

This kind of concern and commitment is very apropos to the present crisis of the poor and unhoused in the twenty-first century. News outlets and editorials show us photographs and tell heart-wrenching stories of families living in streets under overpasses, in cardboard boxes, or in cars and trying to keep warm over heating vents. And the need only seems to grow. This current crisis should be not only a grave concern to Christians everywhere but also a call to action.

Somehow, after catching both the promises and the warnings related to the care of the poor as laid out by the Proverbs writer, we're given a fresh vision of our Christian responsibility to right the wrongs that are shaking the fabric of society.

Jesus, sensitize me to the needs of those around me.
Help me to minister to the poor. Amen.

> **The purposes of a person's heart are deep waters, but one who has insight draws them out.**
>
> —Proverbs 20:5 (NIV)

"I try to put myself in the place of the person I'm reading about in the Bible. Every one of them was a real person." Those words, spoken by the leader of a recent Bible study I attended, caught my attention.

Of course, I know that everyone in the Bible was a real person. Yet I generally skirt over that fact and just note what they said or did. I don't always put myself in their place or ask, "What were they feeling? Why did they react that way? What were their thoughts, fears, hopes, desires, dreams? How would I have felt? What would I have said or done in the same situation?" In the past, I've attempted to find the message but not tried to more fully understand the people who conveyed it.

In my daily life, I'm much the same. Usually I just react, rather than ask myself what a person is feeling or what they might have experienced that prompted their words or actions, especially when I am hurt or angered by them. Too infrequently do I try to put myself in someone else's place.

Author Stephen Covey said, "Seek first to understand." Such good advice, but so poorly have I followed it. Going forward, I'm going to try to place myself in the other person's shoes, both in my Bible reading and in my daily life. I feel certain that if I do, both my understanding and my compassion will increase.

Lord, help me remember there's a reason behind what people say and do. Help me look for and try to understand that reason, both in my study of Your Word and in my life.

—Kim Taylor Henry

Notes

Notes

Notes

LESSON 3: PROVERBS 22:17–31:31

Virtues and Vices

Thank You, Lord, for Your Spirit—and for teaching me the deep things of God. AMEN.

In this third and last lesson on the book of Proverbs we will study a series of fascinating collections—six in all—that are grouped into the last chapters of the book. The introductory verse, or verses, in each collection clues us into the fact that they are separate groups of proverbs. One of these is another great collection of Solomon's proverbs; the other five are often called simply appendices—small collections attached to the main work.

These six collections appear in this order: First we read, "Incline your ear, and hear the words of the wise, and apply your heart to my knowledge" (22:17, ESV). This verse introduces our first series of sayings. Similar introductions are found at 24:23 ("These things also belong to the wise" [NKJV]); at 25:1 (a collection of Solomon's proverbs made by "the men of Hezekiah king of Judah" [NKJV]); at 30:1 ("The words of Agur" [NKJV]); at 31:1 ("The words of King Lemuel" [NIV]); and, finally, the marvelous description of a worthy woman beginning at 31:10 and continuing to the end of the book (31:31).

Let's examine these proverbs in their six separate groups. We begin by looking at the first two collections together.

The Words of the Wise: Choosing Virtue as the Key to Life (22:17–24:34)

Notice first that verses 17 through 21 of chapter 22 give us an extended introduction to this collection of admonitions from the wise teachers of Israel. The introduction speaks of the attitude of the reader or hearer: "Pay attention and turn your ear to the sayings of the wise; apply your heart to what I teach" (22:17, NIV). This is far more than passive hearing; it is active listening. Even though there is wisdom in these proverbs, they are of benefit only if the hearer allows them to affect his will. The Wisdom writer urges us not only to listen but to heed and act.

The introduction then describes the benefits of heeding the teaching. It is "pleasant" to keep or observe these sayings and live by them (22:18, ESV). Furthermore, keeping them will lead us to trust in the Lord (22:19) and live a godly life.

The introduction ends by calling attention to the excellence and truth of the teachings (22:20–21). They are excellent, as the writer has already shown us, because any person who lives by them has a changed will (22:17), a heart filled with the pleasure of right living (22:18), and a life that trusts in God (22:19). As in other biblical teachings, orthodoxy (right teaching) is proved by orthopraxy (right practice). It is by following the teachings that we learn their value.

As we read over these two collections of sayings (22:17–24:22 and 24:23–34), we get the feeling this is just a random assortment. We read about virtues and vices; certain things are praised while others are condemned. Sometimes a saying is repeated in almost the same form—look, for instance, at 22:28 and then read 23:10. Both record the same warning against removing ancient landmarks.

Looking closer, however, we can see that certain themes rise to the surface again and again, reinforcing the idea that strength is in virtue, while evil brings troubles and death. The themes include (1) respect for authority and (2) restraint of the appetites. Both of these ideals of wisdom include important subthemes—compassion for the poor, prudence in public life, and warnings against addiction to alcohol and the life of slothfulness.

Respect for Authority

At several points we will notice that the Wisdom writer pictures himself in a world that is well-ordered—one in which tradition and authority are respected. "The ancient landmark" (ESV, KJV; translated as "boundary stone" in the New International Version) referred to in 22:28 and 23:10 marked the tribal and family landholdings. The wording of these verses is very similar to that found in Deuteronomy 19:14. Even though these boundary markers were easy to move, they were considered sacred. And even though a poor family had not lost title to their land but had in fact lost the use of it through indebtedness, because of ancient tradition they were not to be put off the land that belonged to their ancestors.

In the United States, literary critics have suggested that one special characteristic of Southern writers is a "sense of place." By this they mean that characters in a story have a sense of belonging to a place because they grew up there or because their families, so to speak, have always been in that place. All over the world we find that people often have a strong attachment to a place, even though they may not own a tenth of an acre. The Proverbs writer was in favor of preserving those old attachments that a family has for "place," even though they had become victims of poverty. That is, in effect, the recognition of a kind of authority—the authority of tradition.

The other kind of authority mentioned prominently here is the authority of rulers—political leaders. The emphasis in this section is not so much on obedience to rulers as it is recognizing one's place and how to act when among people who are in authority. For instance, here is some very practical advice about table manners: "When you sit down to dine with a ruler, consider carefully what is before you, and put a knife to your throat if you are a person of great appetite" (23:1–2, NASB).

A further example of how the Proverbs writer respects authority and the order of things is seen at the end of the first collection of sayings: "Fear the Lord and the king, my son, and do not join with rebellious officials, for those two will send sudden destruction on them, and who knows what calamities they can bring?" (24:21–22, NIV).

In a democratic society, our attitude toward political leaders is different from that of a nation ruled and controlled by a dynasty. Our system of government includes provisions for change; change of authority is made a part of the process. But there is still a sense of order. Laws and offices must command a certain respect, or the whole system—and along with it, society—falls into ruin. This is how the proverbs on respect for ruling authorities and ancient boundary stones apply even to us as Christians. The Apostle Paul spoke forthrightly about the importance of our being part of a well-ordered society. Stop a moment and read his instructions to the Christians in Rome about their responsibility to those in authority (Romans 13:1–9).

Restraining the Appetites

Respect for society and the social order are important to the Proverbs writer. But this quality is always coupled with the need to restrain the appetites—our base desires. Personal restraint is a basic ingredient for social harmony as well as for a well-ordered personal life.

Anger is to be restrained. We are to avoid bad-tempered associations. "Do not make friends with a hot-tempered person, do not associate with one easily angered, or you may learn their ways and get yourself ensnared" (22:24–25, NIV). Furthermore, we are not to let pride go unrestrained, because it can lead us into hasty agreements to take on the debts of others (22:26). Haste, pride, and sinful desires lead to many injustices.

We are tempted, out of these kinds of compulsions, for instance, to take advantage of the poor. But the Wisdom writer gives us a stern warning at this point. We are not to rob or oppress the poor in any way or take advantage of their poverty, "For the LORD will plead their case and take the life of those who rob them" (22:23, NASB).

These words in particular cause us to reflect upon the relationship between unrestrained appetite, desires, greed, and the injustices inflicted upon the poor in our "enlightened" modern world. We have to ask ourselves, "Does our affluent society signal a better day for the poor and unhoused people? Or are we more aware of the needs of the less fortunate and destitute people during times of financial and social hardship—periods of recession and depression?"

Some years ago, a newspaper reporter positioned himself in a heavily traveled New York subway station for the sole purpose of observing what kind of people were moved to give money to the impoverished or unhoused people who lined the wall asking for help. Much to his surprise he discovered that it wasn't the well-dressed and obviously well-off people who offered help. Instead, in apparent embarrassment they looked the other way and hurried past the outstretched hands and haunting looks of the hungry and needy. To his amazement he saw that it was those in work clothes—day laborers, domestic workers, etc.—who were more likely to "see" the poor and offer help. Over and over again the Proverbs writer warned that we dare not let our affluence blind us to the needs of others who are less fortunate—especially the poor.

Then, too, here as in other places, the Wisdom writer warns against giving in to the lure of illicit sexual activities. Powerful sex drives are to be restrained and experienced only in ways prescribed by God (see especially 23:26–28). This is an important warning for the Christian of today when sexually explicit movies, television programs, and websites are readily accessible at our very fingertips.

Also included in this part of our scripture lesson are warnings against gluttony and the abuse of alcohol. "For the drunkard and the glutton shall come to poverty: and drowsiness shall clothe a man with rags" (23:21, KJV). The uncontrolled desire for anything, our writer warns, results in a life of disorder and poverty. This truth is vividly illuminated in the next paragraph of our scripture lesson (23:29–35). If you are able to do so, read these seven verses in two or three modern translations as a means of getting the full meaning the original writer wished to convey. (Biblegateway.com and Biblehub.com are helpful places to find multiple translations.)

As you will discover from your reading, we have in these verses perhaps the most famous and colorful of all warnings against the problems of alcohol abuse. In our time, these words carry a profound warning against all forms of addiction, including the abuse of drugs and alcohol for so-called recreational purposes. For the results of addiction to any form of drugs are disastrous physical problems that bring about disorientation and mental confusion, and abnormal and unpredictable behavior of all sorts. This is demonstrated by the devastating toll that opioid addiction has taken on people and families across the United States and around the world.

Miscellaneous and Contrasting Proverbs and Wise Observations

Next, our writer moves from the dangers of alcohol abuse to the tragedy of keeping the wrong company (24:1–10). Again, the description is colorful. We are to avoid being with people whose values reflect a complete disregard for God. And most certainly we are to avoid the corruption of people who in their insatiable thirst for power and position resort to all kinds of gossip and loose talk and who scheme and plot to get their way irrespective of who gets hurt.

The Wisdom writer makes it plain that to associate with unscrupulous people and be envious of them is completely foolish. There is no hope and no future for the undiscriminating person who chooses friends and associates carelessly.

The mood shifts again as the writer gives us a series of contrasting sayings (24:11–22). Again it will be helpful for you to read this section in available modern translations. As we ponder the wisdom contained in these proverbs, two things stand out clearly: "Do not get upset because of evildoers or be envious of the wicked" (24:19, NASB), and "Fear the Lord and the king, my son, and do not join with rebellious officials" (24:21, NIV).

In verses 23 through 29 we are advised of the evils of showing partiality in our relationships; we should be people whose word can be trusted. Then we are urged to be industrious and to be completely fair in our judgment of neighbors and associates. The godly and wise person is neither deceitful nor vindictive.

Finally, in the closing words of chapter 24 we have a vivid picture of the results of laziness, of being slothful (24:30–34). The picture is clear. The writer walked by a field overgrown with weeds and thorns and thistles—even the stone wall was in sad disrepair. It was a disgusting sight. As the writer viewed this scene, the lesson became clear: "A little sleep, a little slumber, a little folding of the hands to rest—and poverty will come on you like a thief and scarcity like an armed man" (24:33–34, NIV).

Practical Lessons

As we ponder thoughtfully this particular part of our scripture (22:17–24:34), certain lessons stand out. The most important part of living wisely is avoiding excess. We are at all times to exercise restraint and not give way to life's baser instincts. Our appetite for excesses of all kinds is to be restrained and curbed. For the Wisdom writers, two virtues are extremely important: humility and industry. Humility is the virtue of not thinking too highly of ourselves. It is the humble person who shows respect for laws and authority.

Industry, on the other hand, is the virtue of giving a good account of our time and work, thereby contributing to the needs of society as a whole. An industrious person is the complete opposite of the lazy person who so grossly neglected his vineyard (24:30–34). The point is this: These two virtues, humility and industry, are essential ingredients of a healthy society and a well-ordered and well-rewarded personal life.

Virtue: Strength for Living

The term *virtue* does not appear as such in the book of Proverbs or the other wisdom writings, but nevertheless the maxims that are threaded throughout the book extol what we understand as virtues—not just the intrinsic goodness of virtue but the result of living a virtuous life, which is the power for living.

The virtues illuminated in these writings are what give us the strength and the insight to confront the realities of life with power. The writer stresses the truth that a lifestyle that leaves God out completely robs a person of strength. By contrast, the pattern of living based on godly virtues supports and strengthens life. Our Proverbs writer pictures this contrast now as he writes, "If you faint in the day of adversity, your strength is small" (24:10, ESV). But then he adds, "My son, eat honey, for it is good; yes, the honey from the comb is sweet to your taste; know that wisdom is the same for your soul; if you find it, then there will be a future, and your hope will not be cut off" (24:13–14, NASB).

Indeed, as Christians our hope is secure in Jesus Christ, the One who was able to completely exemplify the virtues so important to the Proverbs writer. In writing to the Christians in Rome, Paul expressed it so well: "And hope does not put us to shame, because God's love has been poured out into our hearts through the Holy Spirit, who has been given to us. You see, at just the right time, when we were still powerless, Christ died for the ungodly" (Romans 5:5–6, NIV).

The Hezekiah Collection (25:1–29:27)

In the second lesson (Proverbs 10:1 through 22:6) we encountered a group of proverbs that were called "the Proverbs of Solomon." Now, as we move ahead in our lesson, we come to another section that is specifically associated with King Solomon. But in this case our writer says, "These also are proverbs of Solomon which the men of Hezekiah king of Judah copied" (25:1, ESV). King Hezekiah was the thirteenth king of Judah and ruled from around 721 to 693 BC.

According to Jewish tradition, Hezekiah was a patron of the arts, literature, and culture of his people. Another Old

Testament writer tells us that he was faithful to the Lord (2 Kings 18:3–7). He was a contemporary of the prophet Isaiah, who was his adviser and who is considered perhaps the greatest of the literary prophets. It is quite understandable that Hezekiah would have had a special interest in this collection of Proverbs.

An Important Distinction

As we examine this group of proverbs, though, we discover a couple of important distinctions between this collection and the earlier one. In the earlier group, as you will recall, the proverbs were two-part sayings. These are referred to by Bible scholars as *distich*, and some were antithetical in form (A but not B), while others were parallel in form (A and also B).

In this collection we are looking at now, however, we will discover that some of the sayings are three-part—*tristich*, others are four-part—*tetrastich*, and still others are five-part—*pentastich*. An example of a three-part saying is found in 25:8: "Do not go out hastily to argue your case; otherwise, what will you do in the end, when your neighbor humiliates you?" (NASB).

A four-part saying is expressed in these words, "Argue your case with your neighbor himself, and do not reveal another's secret, lest he who hears you bring shame upon you, and your ill repute have no end" (25:9–10, ESV). A five-part saying comes earlier in the chapter: "Do not boast in the presence of the king, and do not stand in the same place as great people; for it is better that it be said to you, 'Come up here,' than for you to be placed lower in the presence of the prince, whom your eyes have seen" (25:6–7, NASB).

A second feature that distinguishes this collection from the earlier group of Solomon's proverbs is that these are more distinctly religious in nature. The earlier ones were practical and almost earthy in tone; these have more to do with religious and ethical themes. The first collection begins with keen observation and draws from that the wisdom of God. This second collection is based upon religious wisdom that is applied to all areas of life.

Of God and the King

The Proverbs writer was very concerned with searching out the proper order of things and determining the difference between that which is highest in value and esteem and that which is lower and less important.

For the most part, those who live in a democratic culture are less preoccupied with order and political station. But we are aware, whether we admit it or not, of the fact that there are various classes or stations within our social structure. And even though we no longer pay tribute to kings and princes, socioeconomic hierarchy is still important to us. How children respect their parents and how we give due honor to public officials and to the laws of our society are as important today as ever. Even more important, the way we view the Lordship of God gives us a particular orientation for all of life.

In these early verses of the "Hezekiah collection," we find the writer bringing together sayings on the place of wisdom with respect to God (25:2a), to the king (25:2b), to the hierarchy of all things (25:3), to the establishment of righteousness in the kingdom (25:4–5), and to the way we should live in humility recognizing and accepting the order of things (25:6–7).

Let's focus on two of these thoughts that will be typical of the themes we will find. First, "It is the glory of God to conceal things, but the glory of kings is to search things out" (25:2, ESV). As the early church father John Chrysostom (circa AD 347–407) is quoted as saying, "A comprehended God is no God." There is just no way we, as finite humans, can even begin to comprehend the One who created the universe. He wouldn't be God if we could understand Him. And an aspect of wisdom is the acceptance of this truth.

The second thought or attitude that is typical of the themes in this section is what might be called "humility." If God is so lofty and unknowable and His understanding far outstrips ours, then our proper attitude must be one of reverence and dependency. Humility is seen by the Hebrew people as an extremely important virtue. It was one of the major characteristics of Moses and it was the reason he could so effectively be used by God. You recall that we defined humility earlier as not thinking more of ourselves than we ought to think; it also means respecting that which is over us—God, the law, public officials, parents, etc.

At the same time, it is important to remember that humility does not involve any form of blind obedience. Throughout our history, heinous crimes have been committed and excused on the basis of "following orders." But authentic biblical humility has nothing to do with a self-justifying attitude. Rather, true humility recognizes and accepts the authority of public leaders, but it also knows there is an even higher authority that transcends everything else.

We have in verses 3 through 7 a description of the ideal king or political leader and the respect that is due such a person. To bring these words into our time and setting is to apply them to any person in a position of leadership—a business executive, a pastor, a store manager. In fact, in this proverb we have a superb New Testament model of "servant-leadership." The model here is not a person who seeks the prominent place, the front-row seat of honor.

It is quite likely that this proverb sparked Jesus's story about the guests at the wedding feast (Luke 14:7–11). You will recall Jesus suggested to His hearers that guests take a lower seat at the table rather than a higher and more prominent seat. This way the host, if he so desired, could invite the guest to move up to a place of higher honor. The point, said Jesus, is that "all those who exalt themselves will be humbled, and those who humble themselves will be exalted" (verse 11, NIV). Compare those words with the words of the Proverbs writer: "For it is better that it be said to you, 'Come up here,' than for you to be placed lower in the presence of the prince, whom your eyes have seen" (Proverbs 25:7, AMP). The point is clear: "Take your place in life by assuming little and giving much. Don't be presumptuous or boast about your abilities or accomplishments. Let others honor you, but don't exalt yourself." That is the essential lesson of true humility. And though that lesson is often lost in our world of aggressive self-promotion, it was seen by the biblical writers as the cornerstone of wise action and of a noble life.

Words for the Good Life

In this next part of our lesson the writer has given us several short, pithy sayings that describe a wholesome lifestyle (25:8–28). The advice given here is just good judgment. In verse 8 we are admonished to not get involved in unnecessary strife, and in verses 9 and 10 we are urged not to involve others in any dispute or argument with neighbors.

Next comes some very practical advice on our manner of speech (25:11–15). The wise person chooses words carefully. There is tremendous power in our words to affect others. The poet expressed it this way: "A word fitly spoken is like apples of gold in pictures of silver. As an earring of gold, and an ornament of fine gold, so is a wise reprover upon an obedient ear" (25:11–12, KJV).

We are then given advice about avoiding excesses (25:16), about never overstaying our welcome (25:17), and about how to treat someone we think of as an enemy. The suggested treatment of enemies certainly goes against the usual pattern: "If your enemy is hungry, give him food to eat; if he is thirsty, give him water to drink. In doing this, you will heap burning coals on his head, and the Lord will reward you" (25:21–22, NIV).

On the surface these words go against the grain, but to act as the Wisdom writer says carries a promise: "the Lord will reward you." How, we ask? Could it be that our reward is the loss of an enemy and the gaining of a friend?

Three Kinds of People Condemned

With colorful language and vivid metaphors, the Wisdom writer now turns his attention to three kinds of people: fools, sluggards (habitually lazy people), and busybodies—meddlers (26:1–28).

In verses 1 through 12 we have a colorful picture of the foolish person. First, foolish people are oblivious to reason; consequently, it is useless to become involved in any kind of conversation with them. Lacking in wisdom, a foolish person is conceited and arrogant, blind to his own lack.

Next, as in earlier proverbs, the slothful or lazy person is condemned (26:13–16). Instead of getting up in the morning and going to work, the lazy man wakes up, turns over, and goes back to sleep (26:14). Verse 15 implies that the slothful person is too lazy even to exert the energy to feed himself. Finally, in verse 16 we have the ludicrous picture of a lazy person who thinks himself wiser and smarter than seven other really competent people. This is certainly one of those places where we get a glimpse of the writer's capacity for exaggeration and humor.

Then comes the condemnation of meddlers or busybodies (26:17–28). We might call them instigators. These troublemakers delight in spreading rumors. They deal in innuendos. Some of them are also practical jokers—they were no more popular in ancient times than they are now (26:18–19). These are insensitive people who are more concerned with their own private enjoyment than they are with the feelings of other people.

The meddlers described in these verses are smooth talkers who enjoy creating dissension, who love to start arguments. And mention is made of the meddler who is motivated by hatred of himself and others yet covers up with flattery and meaningless compliments.

Our instructions are clear. We are not to trust or put any faith in these three kinds of people. We see, too, that to engage in this kind of foolish and deceptive behavior is to invite trouble, for we receive in life what we give.

To read these verses is to realize that human nature has not changed all that much in the well over two thousand years that have passed since these words were recorded. Further, to read these verses without moments of reflection and self-examination is in itself foolish. It is dreadfully easy for us to fall into the traps of being foolish, of being lazy, and of being busybodies—now more than ever, it seems. It is remarkable to see just how relevant and up to date the words of these Wisdom writers are.

Prudence Versus Presumption

As the Wisdom writer moves ahead now, he makes reference to the "prudent" man (27:12). Now, *prudent* is not a word particularly familiar to us in the twenty-first century—it can sound old-fashioned or fussy to our modern ears—but as we check its meaning, we see that it is very relevant to life today: "sensible," "wise," "judicious," and "shrewd."

In this part of our scripture lesson (27:1–27) great emphasis is placed on the value of prudence. In the centuries since the book of Proverbs was collected, philosophers and thinkers have echoed the sentiments we see in these verses. The Roman orator Cicero (106–43 BC) declared that "Prudence is the knowledge of things to be sought, and those to be shunned." *Paradise Lost* author John Milton (1608–1674) defined prudence as "that virtue by which we discern what is proper to be done under the various circumstances of time and place." And philosopher and teacher Amos Bronson Alcott (1799–1888) summed up prudence thusly: "Prudence is the footprint of Wisdom."

A prudent person is one who wisely and carefully plans for the future. Perhaps you know of someone who threw caution to the wind, saying they trusted in God, while doing things that could only be described as unwise or unthinking. This isn't prudence or faith; it is presumption. It is, in effect, deciding for God what He ought to do and then—in the guise of "trusting" Him—demanding that He perform what we expect.

There are other kinds of behavior that relate to presumption. Here the Proverbs writer also speaks of boasting, of envy, and of anger (27:1–4). None of these are characteristic of a wise person.

Humor in the Proverbs

We've already called attention to humor in the book of Proverbs, and we find several humorous notes in chapter 27. Most of us tend to take ourselves too seriously. Consequently, we sometimes fail to see humor in some of the most obvious places. But as we look at this part of our scripture lesson, we can't help but appreciate the sense of humor this Wisdom writer had. There's this proverb, for example: "If anyone loudly blesses their neighbor early in the morning, it will be taken as a curse" (27:14, NIV). This is a wonderful tongue-in-cheek way of saying that even good things, when done at a bad time, will be offensive or off-putting.

There follows a humorous portrait of a nag: "A quarrelsome [spouse] is like the dripping of a leaky roof in a rainstorm; restraining her [or him] is like restraining the wind or grasping oil with the hand" (27:15–16, NIV). The comic depictions of foolishness or impropriety play a significant part in the Wisdom writers' method throughout. Earlier, he recalls the lazy person who gives an absurd excuse for not going to work: "'There is a lion on the road! A lion is in the public square!" (26:13 NASB). Again he speaks of the person who is too lazy to feed himself (26:15). And then there is his graphic description of a meddler as a person who pulls a dog by the ears (26:17).

It is true, of course, that the tone of the book of Proverbs is not the same all the way through. It moves from serious statements of truth to moving depictions of wisdom and folly to comic expressions of the same truth. But it is this frequent appeal to the humorous or comic sense of the absurd that carries us to a greater understanding of truth.

Patience and Haste

A variety of sayings in this great "Hezekiah collection" of Solomon's proverbs is directed mainly toward a person who is willing to work and wait for what is best. These sayings, especially in chapters 28 and 29, encourage us to live deeply, finding our satisfaction not in superficial wealth or doubtful methods of gain but in a life of reverence for God and a desire for wisdom. "Blessed is the one who always trembles before God, but whoever hardens their heart falls into trouble" (28:14, NIV).

It is clear that for the writer, wisdom and righteous living are the qualities that produce strength. "The wicked flee when no one pursues, but the righteous are bold as a lion" (28:1, ESV).

Strength, boldness, and a desire to do the right thing are sometimes related to our willingness to be patient, to exercise restraint in our actions and words: "A faithful person will abound with blessings, but one who hurries to be rich will not go unpunished" (28:20, NASB). A similar warning against haste reads, "The stingy are eager to get rich and are unaware that poverty awaits them" (28:22, NIV).

Wise Persons Guard Their Words

Warning is given in this section, too, about the importance of using restraint in the use of words. For example, "A [short-sighted] fool always loses his temper and displays his anger, but a wise man [uses self-control and] holds it back" (29:11, AMP). Scripture shows us the value of words—they are to be used wisely.

In our society today we are bombarded with words—in conversation, in emails and texts, on radio and television, and in print. The internet and social media have given people unprecedented ways in which to express themselves and their views, and to share intimate details of their lives. In the midst of all this, we have failed to see the importance sometimes of *not* speaking, of withholding our opinion. Consequently, we often fall into the trap of speaking or writing superficially without giving thought to what we should say—and what might best be left unsaid.

Wisdom and the Public Good

It is quite natural that in this collection of Proverbs that Hezekiah's people copied we should find frequent allusion to the value of wisdom and righteousness in public life. Of great concern to both Solomon and Hezekiah were the general health of society, the prudence of political and national leaders, and the loyalty of citizens. Both Solomon and Hezekiah were interested in good government and a peaceful and productive society.

We have frequent warnings here against evil and sinful rulers or political leaders (see 28:15–16; also 29:2, 4, 12). On the other hand, the political leader who is just, honest, and considerate is assured of a happy tenure (see 29:14, 18). Again, we see that the centuries have not witnessed a change in basic truth. When political leaders in our twenty-first-century world have integrity and are honest and just, the results are peace, harmony, and happiness in our national life. But we've also seen the payoff when national and regional leaders are corrupt and deceitful in their struggle for power and position in a disillusioned electorate.

Agur's Wisdom (30:1–33)

The Agur Mystery

As we progress in our studies through chapter 30, we become aware of how distinct this material is from anything else we've encountered so far in the book of Proverbs. To begin with, we read, "The words of Agur the son of Jakeh, even the prophecy" (30:1, KJV). We have no idea who Agur is, or Jakeh, except that Bible scholars do not identify these as Hebrew names. Agur is mentioned nowhere else in the Bible, but it is likely he was a wise man of some note and possibly an Arab. In Jewish tradition, Agur is taken to be a pen name for Solomon, but this presupposition is not accepted by modern scholars.

The Agur mystery is deepened further by the words "The man declares to Ithiel, to Ithiel and Ucal" (30:1, NASB). While Ithiel appears as a proper name in Nehemiah 11:7, we cannot be certain these are proper names as translated here. Like some other English translations, the English Standard Version's rendering of verse 1 omits any mention of Ithiel and Ucal and reads, "The man declares, I am weary, O God; I am weary, O God, and worn out," and it is possible that the original Hebrew consonants here could be understood to read, "I have wearied myself, O God, I have wearied myself, O God, and I am at my wit's end."

A Skeptic Speaks and Asks Questions

This latter translation is feasible based on the mood of the next three verses. Indeed Agur appears to be at his wit's end. These are the words of a skeptic who freely admits that he lacks understanding and wisdom and cannot comprehend "the Holy One" (30:3, NIV). As further evidence of Agur's quandary, he asks several rhetorical questions in verse 4: "Who has ascended into heaven and descended? Who has gathered the wind in His fists? Who has wrapped the waters in His garment? Who has established all the ends of the earth? What is His name or His Son's name? Surely you know!" (NASB).

In response to Agur's somewhat cynical statements and questions, we are given the response of a wise man of faith: "Every word of God is pure [tried and found true]: he is a shield unto them that put their trust in him" (30:5, KJV). Another way to translate those words is "Every word of God is flawless" (NIV).

Psalm 12:6 concurs: "And the words of the Lord are flawless, like silver purified in a crucible, like gold refined seven times" (NIV). Centuries later, the Apostle Paul echoed this declaration in 2 Timothy 3:16: "All Scripture is God-breathed and is useful for teaching, rebuking, correcting and training in righteousness" (NIV). That's the way it was with the Wisdom writer; the Word of God is true because it proves itself in practical experience. For this reason God's Word is a refuge (30:5) and is sufficient for our needs (30:6).

Things Never Fully Satisfied

The Wisdom writer moves now into a series of numerical proverbs. He opens this section with these words, "The leech has two daughters: 'Give' and 'Give'" (30:15, NASB). The reference here is undoubtedly to a bloodsucking variety of leech that was common in Palestine at that time. We don't know the original intention, but it is possible these words give us a colorful picture of the nature of greed and the spirit of dissatisfaction. This seems quite plausible because he next comments on four things that are never fully satisfied: "the grave, the barren womb, land, which is never satisfied with water, and fire, which never says, 'Enough!'" (30:16, NIV). Most certainly, greed, dissatisfaction, and uncontrolled desires are destructive to the human personality.

Things That Are Wonderful and Treacherous, Loved and Despised

The words of Agur list a great variety of observations about manners and morals, respect for those who are over us, and justice toward those who are under us. The inventiveness of the words, the intriguing association of thoughts and images pull us into what he is saying. We are not likely to forget "Three things are too wonderful for me; four I do not understand" (30:18, ESV). He then goes on to list them: "the way of an eagle in the sky, the way of a snake on a rock, the way of a ship on the high seas, and the way of a man with a young woman" (30:19, NIV).

Obviously the punch line in this list of "wonderful things" is the way of a man with a young woman. We will have to remember that courtship was carried out quite differently in those days: It was briefer and not as open to the public. The eagle, the snake, and the ship leave no trace of their progress, and similarly, no trace of the courtship can be seen until the marriage is announced. Even today, the progress of "falling in love" and subsequent courtship leaves us mystified at the power of love to bring two people into the commitment of marriage.

By contrast, the behavior of the adulterous woman is one of unconcern without commitment. Her sexual escapades are as casual as eating a meal. Our writer pictures a sexually promiscuous woman in these words: "This is the way of an adulteress: she eats and wipes her mouth and says, 'I have done no wrong'" (30:20, ESV). Quite a contrast with "the way of a man with a maid" (verse 19, KJV)!

Four Impossible Kinds of People

Agur next comments on four kinds of people who can create havoc in society and cause disturbing imbalances (30:21–23). First, there is the servant who without ability or preparation and probably through treachery ascends to a place of leadership; a fool with a full stomach; a married woman who is unloved; and a servant-maid who takes the place of her mistress in the master's affections. In each of these, there is the assumption of deceit and treachery.

Four Minor but Very Wise Animals

To highlight the truth that wisdom is sometimes found in strange places, here are models of wisdom that people would do well to emulate (30:24–28): ants, hyraxes (also known as conies or rock badgers), locusts, and lizards (most recent translations) or spiders (KJV, among others). Only a very wise, observant, and insightful writer would see the characteristics of wisdom in these "low" forms of animal life. He sees the ant as the model of busyness and planning for the future; the badger is a master builder; locusts are models of orderliness and discipline; and the spider or lizard is a model of overcoming handicaps and can climb any wall, even that of "kings' palaces" (NIV).

For people in ancient Israel as well as for us in the twenty-first century, there are valuable clues to the meaning and wisdom of life in the world of nature. This thread doesn't run through the book of Proverbs as much as it does in the Psalms where we have magnificent poems exalting nature as the handiwork of God (see Psalm 19).

Four Impressive Things

Agur concludes this listing of numerical proverbs by drawing attention to four impressive things: a lion, a greyhound (later translations refer to a strutting cock or rooster), a male goat, and a king who is in complete control (30:29–31). While the full intent of this proverb may not be entirely clear, the reference seems to be to intelligent leadership and a stable government. The Proverbs writer has already warned against oppressive and unjust governments, but here he seems to be acknowledging the virtue of a strong and reliable political structure.

The Need for Self-Restraint

The Agur section closes with some wise words about the importance of self-control (verse 33). Readers are urged to avoid being pushy and arrogant. The wise person doesn't continually sound off about his or her abilities because this creates trouble and produces bad results comparable to sour milk ("butter," NIV, or "curds," ESV) or a bloody nose that comes from being hit or twisted.

While certain of the images found in this Agur section were very familiar to its first readers, they are a bit more obscure to us. But as we reflect on his warnings and four-part sayings, we find wise instruction for our day-to-day activities and relationships with other people.

King Lemuel's Instruction (31:1–9)

Here we have an unknown king repeating the wise words of instruction taught him by his mother. Briefly, this king learned three important things to properly handle his leadership role. First, he was to avoid illicit sexual encounters. Second, he was not to allow himself to become befuddled and confused by indulging in "intoxicating drink" (NASB). If a person of responsibility, such as a political leader, judge, doctor, or lawyer, abuses alcohol, he or she risks failure in the performance of duty. Third, the wise leader defends the rights of the "poor and needy" (31:9, ESV). Again and again throughout the Bible and especially in this book of Proverbs, the acid test of leadership is the care given to the "have-nots"—the poor.

The Strength of a Wise Woman (31:10–31)

These closing words of the book of Proverbs are well-known to many and much loved. They are in the form of an acrostic poem—each line begins with a letter of the Hebrew alphabet, beginning with *aleph* (the first) and ending with *taw* (the last). This means there are twenty-two couplets descriptive of a wise woman, a capable wife.

The description opens with these words: "Who can find a virtuous woman? for her price is far above rubies." Here again the use of the word *virtuous* carries not just the idea of goodness or uprightness but also strength. The virtuous woman is one who knows how to live. She exerts strength as she works diligently for her family (31:13–15; 31:17–19), and she is adept at making wise business decisions (31:16).

Through this wise woman's efforts her entire family profits (31:21), and her husband's success as a leader is the result of her industry and prudence. In verse 23 we read that her husband is "known in the gates" (KJV). Ancient Near Eastern cities were walled and the "gate" was the place where the elders or city fathers met to conduct official public business. It was an official place comparable to our courthouse or state house. In other words, with his wife's help, he was a prominent public figure.

Another characteristic of this wise woman is that even though she is heavily involved with the welfare of her family, she is sensitive to the needs of the poor in her community (31:20). And in verse 26 we read, "She opens her mouth with wisdom, and the teaching of kindness is on her tongue" (ESV). She doesn't spend her time gossiping or criticizing but speaks with wisdom, restraint, and kindness.

Among the most beautiful and moving accolades offered this woman are these: "Her children arise and call her blessed; her husband also, and he praises her: 'Many women do noble things, but you surpass them all'" (31:28–29, NIV). We are blessed indeed if we had the opportunity to learn wisdom and virtue from our mothers.

This poetic tribute closes on a profoundly spiritual note: "Charm is deceitful and beauty is vain, but a woman who fears the LORD, she shall be praised. Give her the product of her hands, and let her works praise her in the gates" (31:30–31, NASB).

The test of authentic wisdom for this woman and for people of all times is devotion to God. And for us in a technological world that the Wisdom writers could never have pictured in their wildest imaginations, the test of our wisdom is the same as our ancient counterparts: devotion to God and to His Son, Jesus Christ.

*Father, let me open my mouth with wisdom;
let others find in my words the law of kindness.* AMEN.

A LIZARD IN THE PALACE

A lizard can be caught with the hand, yet it is found in kings' palaces.

—Proverbs 30:28 (NIV)

For years, an anole lizard lived in the foliage of the wreath on my front door. I always looked for it when I returned home. Mr. Lizard, as I affectionately named him, would peek his head around the plastic leaves of the wreath that kept him safe. At least five separate times, that lizard made his way into our house. He'd scurry through the open front door, or he'd cling to the wreath when I switched it out seasonally. Each time, I would carefully check our decorations and take him back outside to the new wreath.

  I loved that little lizard because he became an unlikely resident of our home. The proverb above is powerful for a similar reason. Can you imagine lizards living among the splendor of kings? As this verse states, lizards can be caught by ordinary human hands. Yet they were found in palaces—and I imagine they still can be to this day. We each, like lizards, have the opportunity to make our dwelling a royal one. When we climb the walls that have held back our God-granted giftings, we will find ourselves in His kingdom full of opportunities.

Lord Jesus, like the lizard that is ordinary but makes his home among kings and queens, help me to see the opportunities You've given me to dwell among royalty, for you are the King of kings.

—Ashley Clark

Notes

Notes

Notes

LESSON 4: ECCLESIASTES 1–4

The Mystery of Life

Lord, I commit my life to You. Teach me Your way. AMEN.

Does Anything Really Matter? (1:1–11)

"The words of the Preacher" stand in relationship to other books of the Bible as a question mark to a period or an exclamation point (1:1a). Most of the time, truth is given to us in declarative statements: "In the beginning God created the heavens"; or "God is love"; or yet again, "No one has seen God at any time." Sometimes truth appears to us in an imperative form: "Thou shalt love the LORD thy God"; or "Thou shalt not kill."

But sometimes truth is best served by a tough, realistic, and probing question. Here the writer questions the real purpose of life with his declaration, "Vanity of vanities . . . all is vanity" (1:2, ESV). Other translations render "vanity" as "Meaningless! . . . Everything is meaningless!" or "Futility of futilities . . . All is futility." At each point we find him testing life by his central question: Does anything really matter? Or is everything emptiness, a vapor that disappears, a labor that ends in disappointment, a striving after the wind?

A Voice from the Past
Most students of Ecclesiastes believe the book was written sometime after the Babylonian exile, possibly in the fourth or

third century BC. The Hebrew in which the book is written is characteristic of that late post-exilic period, and it is very different from the earlier style of the language.

Koheleth (the Hebrew word translated as the "Preacher" or "Teacher") is introduced to us, however, as "the son of David, king of Jerusalem" (1:1, KJV). Immediately we see that this refers to Solomon, a man who, in the tradition of Israel, would have had opportunity to know all of the best life had to offer. If wealth would bring happiness and purpose to life, then he, who was perhaps the wealthiest of Israel's monarchs, could have known its possibilities. If wisdom would satisfy, then who could better judge its qualities than the one to whom God had granted an unusual measure? And if pleasure is an answer to life's longings, then here was a king whose properties included all that would delight the senses.

That is why the writer evokes the memory of this king and uses him as the "voice" who poses the question: Aren't all these things really empty and meaningless? We know that is what the writer is doing when he says in verse 12, "I the Preacher have been king over Israel in Jerusalem" (ESV). The Ecclesiastes writer wrote the book many centuries after the time of Solomon. Solomon, of course, wouldn't have referred to himself as king in the past tense! But the Wisdom writer knew that his contemporary reader would understand: This essay on the meaning of life was written from the point of view of the well-known historical character. We are right to think of him as Solomon; this is what the writer had in mind when he explored the great questions of the mystery of life.

Does Anything Ever Change?

These questions are primary to the Ecclesiastes writer: If nothing really changes in this world, and if everything finally comes around full circle and ends in the dust of death, does it really matter what we do and how we live? Are all of our efforts lost in the great unchanging, steady state of the universe? The Preacher saw that the problem of whether life itself is an empty exercise or an adventure with genuine purpose hinged on these questions.

He expressed the great dilemma of life in its most devastating and difficult form. What good does it do, he asked in effect, for a person to work, strive, and aspire to achieve something (see 1:3)? After all, he says, "Generations come and generations go, but the earth remains forever. The sun rises and the sun sets, and hurries back to where it rises" (1:4–5, NIV).

When the writer looks at the world around him, he sees perfect order—in fact, order that is too perfect. The perfect circle is his picture of nature and the life he observes. The wind and the rivers run their courses, but then they simply return to the place where they began (1:6–7). The world is full of energy and force and activity—but it all ends up in the same way. There is nothing new; everything returns to the same point on the perfect circle of existence.

It is an interesting fact of human existence that we have trouble relating to anything that is too perfect. Art critics say that a work that is too symmetrical, too perfect, is simply dull and uninteresting. In music and poetry we must sometimes be surprised by an irregularity in the rhyme and rhythm; otherwise we do not enjoy it. Regularity is important, and organization is part of its beauty, but what makes something a work of art is that touch that distinguishes it and makes it unique.

Novelty for the sake of novelty is not art either, of course. The irregular that is nothing but irregularity calls for the humdrum sameness and consistency that the Preacher spoke about. Variety is the spice of life, but even variety depends upon a perceptible pattern. By the same token, humor is not humorous unless there is a certain reasonableness about it; the plausibility of the humor is what makes the punch line work. But, on the other hand, the punch line cannot be entirely predictable; it must be a surprise—something new "under the sun."

We will do well to remember, in contrast to what the Preacher complained about, that regularity provides us with both pleasure and comfort. It was that attractive sense of the new and different that the Preacher missed when he looked out at the broad picture of life. Things may appear to be new, he says, but in fact we've only forgotten—they have all happened before. One generation moves on and another comes along. The cycle of life repeats itself. Our writer words it this way: "What has been will be again, what has been done will be done again; there is nothing new under the sun" (1:9, NIV). Then to complete the Preacher's rather melancholy view of life, he says in effect in verse 11 that people in the past are not remembered and people now will not be remembered by those who follow after.

The Desire for Meaning (1:12–18)

As we have learned in our lessons up to this point, the search for wisdom was extremely important to the people of the ancient Near East and to the people of Israel—especially the aristocratic class headed by the king. In Israel, Solomon was the "patron saint" of the wisdom movement, but King Hezekiah also figured prominently in it. And the wisdom movement flourished when the exiles returned to Judah after their years in Babylon in the sixth and fifth centuries BC.

Because of Solomon's role as the founder of Israel's wisdom school, our writer, the Preacher, took on the identity of Solomon to illustrate the idea that even kingly wisdom and power are insufficient to change things. And when he spoke of his inner longing—"And I applied my heart to seek and to search out by wisdom all that is done under heaven" (1:13, ESV)—he was beginning to openly express his concern over what appears to be the everlasting sameness of things.

In spite of the eternal striving of people everywhere, the Preacher had discovered nothing new. There is a great all-encompassing regularity to the ways of the world. Yet he had also discovered that down deep inside there is "this heavy burden God has laid on mankind!" (1:13, NIV). While the pattern of nature seems to be endless repetition, the deep longing of the human heart is for a goal, a purpose, a meaning.

Viktor Frankl, the Viennese psychiatrist, wrote a book entitled *Man's Search for Meaning* in which he described in vivid detail his experience as a prisoner of the Nazi regime during World War II. Among many things, he told how he wanted to discover what was different about those prisoners who, even against heavy odds, survived the prison camp experience. One of the most common traits of the survivors was that they had a reason to live beyond their time in prison. The reason might take on different forms, but whatever it was, it gave meaning and purpose to life. Frankl later concluded that, as it was for these survivors, the desire for meaning in life is a fundamental psychological need.

A Goal and a Purpose

But when we say that something has meaning, we also imply that it has a goal and a purpose. We mean that it is going somewhere and that something "new" is anticipated from the experience.

This is the "heavy burden" that the Preacher speaks about and that causes him to react with such passion against the eternal sameness of things. If things are always the same, then the future holds nothing really new or exciting. And if that is the case, then life has no purpose, no meaning. We are all dressed up, and we have nowhere to go.

Can it be true, then, the writer asks, that reality is at cross purposes with the longings of the human heart? If we rely upon what can be searched out by wisdom and observation, then that is all we can find. "I have seen all the works that are done under the sun," he wrote, "and, behold, all is vanity [emptiness] and vexation of spirit" (1:14, KJV). More recent translations render this phrase as variations of "meaningless, a chasing after the wind" (NIV).

On one hand, all our experiences are empty and, like a vapor, disappear without a trace. That is vanity—futility or meaninglessness. And on the other hand, there is this longing for purpose—the "chasing after the wind" he refers to.

Moreover, since wisdom could not change this condition, the problem was intensified by the knowledge of the unsolvable conflict: A person hopes, plans, and anticipates—but his or her striving meets the solid resistance of a world that swallows up novelty, dashes hopes, and makes a mockery of all who think that their labor and earnest striving have any meaning. As the Preacher saw it, the eternal sameness is unalterable, so consequently, there can be no hope. The human heart, as wisdom reveals to the writer, is at odds with reality. And there seems to be no cure. "What is crooked cannot be straightened, and what is lacking cannot be counted. I said to myself, 'Behold, I have magnified and increased wisdom more than all who were over Jerusalem before me; and my mind has observed a wealth of wisdom and knowledge'" (1:15–16, NASB).

But as we examine this condition, what is the answer that wisdom gives? His initial response follows immediately: "And I applied my heart to know wisdom and to know madness and folly. I perceived that this also is but a striving after wind. For in much wisdom is much vexation, and he who increases knowledge increases sorrow" (1:17–18, ESV). What an amazingly gloomy outlook!

Though we might expect or hope otherwise, the question he poses does not become easily resolved in the remainder of the book of Ecclesiastes. In fact, if anything, the questions become sharper and more critical. All of this forces us to consider the human condition that we live with, and for which there are no easy answers.

The fact that there may be answers, however, is hinted at all along. And though the answer itself is not given, the very feature of this book that causes it to always make reference to God is significant. Though the doubts that we find expressed here are as strong as any we find in the Bible, they can hardly be thought of as the doubts of a nonbeliever. After all, the questions are directed to God, and He is named no fewer than thirty-seven times in Ecclesiastes. The Preacher's admission of the great mystery of life is, in a sense, a confession of the greatness of God.

Is Pleasure a Way of Escape? (2:1–11)

As we move into this part of our scripture lesson, we see that the Preacher has moved beyond the purely intellectual point of view of the questions that he has been asking. If we live with this condition that stumps us mentally, can we escape or bypass the intellectual response altogether? Can we simply turn our energies to the pursuit of pleasure?

Here, as at many points, our writer sounds like a modern existentialist philosopher. Author Albert Camus, for instance, retold the ancient story of Sisyphus, who was condemned by the gods to roll a stone up a hill, only to have it roll back down again and again and again. Camus pointed to the meaninglessness of this task as a symbol of life, just as the Preacher spoke of the meaninglessness of human striving. But Camus insisted that a person is most human when he, like Sisyphus, places his shoulder against the stone, grits his teeth, and (as if the condition of meaningless life did not exist) begins to roll it again to the top of the hill.

In response to this problem, the Preacher now wrote, "I said to myself, 'Come now, I will test you with pleasure to find out what is good.' But that also proved to be meaningless" (2:1). Put another way, "I said to myself, 'I will turn to pleasure for answers,' but I learned there weren't any."

Modern commentators of the social scene often draw a connection between the fact that we live in a world that is adrift, with no purpose and no meaning, and the high incidence of drug and alcohol abuse. These are related, they say, because a world without meaning invites us to pursue some means of escape from the intolerable sense of purposelessness.

Is This Really the Answer?

But the Preacher says that the escape route of pleasure doesn't work. Instead of giving himself to the excesses of wine, he kept himself under control: "I searched with my heart how to cheer my body with wine—my heart still guiding me with wisdom" (2:3, ESV). Rather than living the life of a completely unprincipled person who wanted only to escape, he kept intellectually alert to the real effect of what he was doing. Observing this course of action, he asked, in effect, "Is this really an answer?"

There are many pleasures that we can escape into. For some, drink and drugs, along with other kinds of folly, are the more direct ways of escape (2:3). Others, as the Preacher realized, escape into their work and become workaholics (2:4) and bask in their accomplishments (2:5–9). And he said, "I denied myself nothing my eyes desired; I refused my heart no pleasure. My heart took delight in all my labor, and this was the reward for all my toil" (2:10, NIV).

The Wrong Answers

In this part of our scripture lesson (2:4–10), the Ecclesiastes writer probably touched on the most frequent means of escape. After all, as great as the problem of drug and alcohol abuse might be, most of us live our lives free of that kind of addiction. Most of us live productively and sensibly, doing our work and accumulating material gain. These things, in fact, preoccupy us so much that we seldom stop to ask if they provide answers to the deepest longings of the human heart or to the real needs of the world we live in. On a day-to-day basis most of us live *as if* there is meaning and purpose in our lives, but, in reality, we've not really confronted the question of life's deepest meaning. But the benefit of the book of Ecclesiastes for us is that it wakes us up to the emptiness of pleasure, work, and gain as the means of discovering wholeness in life.

Verse 11 is the conclusion of this section. Here we see that the Preacher reflected on all that he had done and experienced. Our image here is of a man, advanced in age, who can now be somewhat detached from his former preoccupation so that he realistically measures the value of his accomplishments. And as he does this, his words drip with disappointment. "Yet when I surveyed all that my hands had done and what I had toiled to achieve, everything was meaningless, a chasing after the wind; nothing was gained under the sun" (2:11, NIV). What a tragic epitaph!

In recent decades, sociologists and psychologist have observed two topics of public concern that raise issues similar to the writer's findings here. One is the condition that scientists have called "workaholism." For the workaholic, work becomes an addiction; it is a way of escaping from life. It rescues us from the tensions of normal relationships or of honest self-appraisal. Work becomes, for us who are workaholics, the "world." Rather than a means toward an end, it becomes the end. But here our writer wakes us up to the reality that this is a false end—it is like chasing the wind, a flood of effort without profit.

The other contemporary concern is the disorder we call "burnout." To say that we are "burned out" with our jobs, our family obligations, or our various roles in life is to admit that these things no longer hold any interest for us. We feel like we are on a hopeless treadmill. We're running hard but getting nowhere. Burnout is, in a way, the discovery in our personal experience of what the Preacher meant when he said, "And behold, all was vanity and a striving after wind, and there was nothing to be gained under the sun" (2:11, ESV).

Wisdom and Folly (2:12-17)

Earlier we saw (1:12–18) that as the Preacher was wrestling with the value of wisdom, he arrived at the conclusion that wisdom put him in touch, more than ever, with the central irony of life: Though we feel a strong desire to expend effort toward some worthy end, the world itself yields nothing new and our efforts make no difference. Consequently, as he sees it, to acquire wisdom is to know even greater conflict and pain. Now, in this part of our scripture lesson, he turns his attention to a somewhat different question: Is wisdom, after all, better than folly?

We might rephrase his question this way: Are we better off knowing or not knowing? Does wisdom hold some intrinsic value that proves itself by enriching our lives, even though it brings greater pain and disturbs our minds?

What Is Better?

The Preacher introduces the question slowly and carefully, holding it up as an object of serious inquiry: "So I turned to consider wisdom, insanity, and foolishness; for what will the man do who will come after the king, except what has already been done?" (2:12, NASB). Put simply, the Ecclesiastes writer—based on his growing conviction that "there is nothing new under the sun" (1:9, NIV) and our efforts do not really change anything much—is asking himself whether wisdom has more to offer than folly. Why choose the painful and disturbing way of wisdom over the less painful way of folly or foolishness?

A Cynical Response

At first he seems to answer the question positively: "Then I saw that there is more gain in wisdom than in folly, as there is more gain in light than in darkness" (2:13, ESV). But even as he says that, we catch the tone of irony in his voice. For he goes on to say that when the chips are down, a wise person who has put up with all the strain and pain that go with acquiring wisdom is no better off than a foolish person who has "gone with the flow" and has taken the easy way. As he sees it, the same fate awaits both the wise person and the foolish person—both die and are soon forgotten (2:14–16). Consequently, he decides that life isn't really worthwhile. "So

I hated life"—because living is just a lot of trouble . . . it is empty and like chasing after the wind, and there is no lasting purpose (2:17, NIV).

Why Bother?

It is this attitude that seems to pervade the thinking of many people in our twenty-first-century world. Why bother with the pain of confronting the roots of the drug problem or the problems of the unhoused or the impoverished if they seem unwilling to help themselves? There have always been people like that in our world and there always will be. It is like "chasing the wind" to worry about them, and besides, we all meet a common fate; we all die and are soon forgotten. Meanwhile, the world goes on the same way.

But we have an advantage not shared by the writer of Ecclesiastes because we live on this side of the Cross. The life, death, and resurrection of Jesus rule out our being oblivious to the deep meanings of life in this world—to the strain and pain of living creatively in the "footsteps of Jesus," and of loving our neighbor and caring what happens to him or her.

The Perplexity of Life and Death (2:18–23)

The Preacher moves now from his belief that life isn't worthwhile—"I hated life"—to the thought that his work isn't worthwhile—"I hated all the fruit of my labor" (2:18, NASB). After all, if we all die anyway, what difference does it make if we work hard and scrimp and save? Why struggle and work to build a fortune and then leave it to an heir who may handle it foolishly? Such questions focus on two realities that increase the perplexity of life for the Preacher.

First, the writer recognizes that there is a limit to what and how much we can do, and there are limits to the control we can exercise over the results of our labor. "You can't take it with you" is a cliché we've all heard many times. Such being the case, the Preacher decries the idea of working and sweating to build up a reserve that a child or heir may squander. Since death is the end for the Preacher, why struggle for something he can't control?

The second reality our writer faces is that he cannot predict the future. Of course, we build in all the safeguards that we can, but in truth the future is elusive, and the distant future is even more elusive. If the Preacher thought life was beyond his control and robbed him of any satisfaction, how much more was death beyond his control, so why bother to work hard? The extent of his despair is seen in these words: "What do people get for all the toil and anxious striving with which they labor under the sun? All their days their work is grief and pain; even at night their minds do not rest. This too is meaningless" (2:22–23, NIV).

Limits and Freedom (2:24–26)

In our study so far, we have learned that the Preacher had a tragically dismal view of life. He most certainly wasn't a positive or possibility thinker. We've all known people who were like the Preacher to varying degrees. They're just not fun to be around. To put it mildly, the Preacher was a dyed-in-the-wool pessimist, a doom-and-gloom thinker of the worst kind.

A Ray of Hope

But now we get our first hint that his view of life wasn't completely dismal. And I say just a hint because he still wasn't ready to give us answers to the puzzling ambiguities of life. But he does give us a glimmer of hope in these words: "A person can do nothing better than to eat and drink and find satisfaction in their own toil" (2:24, NIV).

This is not, as we might first assume, simple hedonism—an abandonment to pleasure wherever it can be found. The Preacher had already rejected that possibility (2:1–11). Instead, he is saying that there is some good in the possibility of receiving and rejoicing in what *we do have,* without asking for more. After all, what we do have is "from the hand of God."

Accepting Limits

We tend to underestimate how important this idea—accepting one's limits—was to Old Testament people. There is great satisfaction, as we can all know, in accepting certain limits. A maturing process takes place when we face the fact that we will not fulfill *all* our childhood dreams—that these dreams need to be transformed and modified by the real limits of time, resources, and possibilities. When we are young, we think of many possibilities. But as we live, we fasten upon a particular career, a particular mate, and a certain home with a very specific address. We don't give up our dreams easily, but bringing some dreams into reality often means letting others die. Otherwise we live in our world of wishes, which turns into a bitter rebellion against the world that *is.* We must live with our limits in order to live at all.

We mature further when we learn to face the limits of our abilities, our vocation, and life itself, which ends in death. In fact, when the Preacher spoke of death, he was referring, in a sense, to the whole subject of limits in life. And in many ways the very power to live, and to live a life free from overwhelming fear, is made possible by the acceptance of death as a reality in life.

Our writer's understanding of death and the resurrection of the dead was undoubtedly different from New Testament understanding today. But even in the New Testament, we don't find a view of life after death that is a mere assurance of survival. Death is still a mystery, and everything beyond death is in God's hands. The comfort of New Testament teaching comes from the knowledge that God's love transcends death, and that the mystery of God is greater than the prospect of death.

In that sense, the Preacher is saying the same thing. We cannot know everything, he says, and we cannot escape the apparent contradictions in life. Our questions are useful only up to a certain point, beyond which they are useless—but beyond *that* is God!

So it is within that limitation that we have the freedom not to strive against life but to receive it and enjoy it.

The Seasons of Life (3:1–8)

Ancient people had a sense of time that was not totally dominated by the clock. Our sense of time tends to be of time running in linear fashion from a remote beginning to an unknown future; it is measured in seconds, minutes, hours, days, and years. In other words, it is measured by abstract calculations of time, and it is basically abstract time.

Kinds of Time

In contrast, ancient people like the Hebrews were always strongly drawn toward a much more concrete picture of time. There were kinds of time: time that "belonged" to some event, time that was marked, not by abstract measures but by real historical happenings—the birth of a baby, the harvest of a crop, the creation of the world.

A Rhythm in Life

In this beautiful poem on "the times" that makes up our scripture lesson now (3:1–8), we are given a feeling of time filled up with events—events that recur. There is a rhythm in life. And in many ways this rhythm is a source of comfort and even joy. Like family traditions at Thanksgiving, Christmas, and the Fourth of July, we enjoy the repetition.

It is true that in our better moments we may say "variety is the spice of life," but in reality, we also like doing the same thing over and over again. A world of order and predictability is a familiar world, a comfortable world, a safe world—a "friendly" world.

A Comfortable Rhythm

This is the feeling we get when we read about the "kinds of time" the Preacher speaks of in our scripture lesson. Listed here is a series of opposite and complementary events. Each of these events has its own time, "a time to be born, and a time to die; a time to plant, and a time to pluck up that which is planted" (3:2, KJV). The alternating times are given their place and their season: "A time to kill, and a time to heal; a time to break down, and a time to build up; a time to weep, and a time to laugh; a time to mourn, and a time to dance . . . a time to embrace, and a time to refrain from embracing; a time to get, and a time to lose; a time to keep, and a time to cast away; a time to rend, and a time to sew; a time to keep silence, and a time to speak."

As the Preacher said earlier, "There is a time for everything, and a season for every activity under the heavens" (3:1, NIV). The rhythm is comforting; these events are familiar; they have all happened before and they will happen again. None of them is a stranger to us. It is a friendly world.

But our writer's purpose in this poem is not to emphasize this feeling of familiarity and order; he wants to say something else that is very important.

A Restricting Rhythm

This kind of order is also a restriction because our lives are circumscribed by the repetition of events. We live on a wheel of preordained and repeating events. There is nothing really new, nothing to anticipate that has not already happened. Experience is a recollection—one generation knows only what former generations have already known.

The Wheel of Misfortune (3:9–22)

Though we gain comfort—the comfort of an old friend, familiar faces, remembered circumstances, and predictable good cheer—from repetition, we also feel the need to rise above it. That is why, on the one hand, this poem (3:1–8) is quoted so often for its beauty and comfort, yet the Preacher himself puts it to a very different use. We begin to see his purpose in evoking the thoughts of cycles and repetitions and the great wheel of time, as we look at this next part of our scripture lesson.

If we follow the rhythm of this great wheel of time—from birth to death, from war to peace and back again (3:1–8)—where does it take us? Always back to the beginning. In the final analysis, a circle goes nowhere. Wheels may take us somewhere, but only if we use them to ride in a straight line.

It is important for each of us to ascertain whether we are on the wheel of history that is moving forward to new experiences and to some ultimate goal, or whether the wheel we are on *is* history. There is a vast difference between the two. If we are on the wheel that *is* history, we monotonously go round and round, never actually getting anywhere. It is on this wheel that the Preacher is most comfortable, and this explains why he is unable to discover purpose in a life that is limited by death. "All are of the dust, and all turn to dust again" (3:20, KJV).

But the Preacher tells us that even within these limits, there is the possibility of doing good and of finding "satisfaction in all [our] toil"—for these are the gifts of God (3:12–13, NIV). We cannot get above this wheel of history, the writer insists, simply because this world of cycles is the only perspective human beings have: "He has also set eternity in the human heart; yet no one can fathom what God has done from beginning to end" (3:11, NIV). In other words, God has implanted in us a passion to understand time—the past and future—but we do not know, as the Preacher sees it, how God controls the seasons or whether there is meaning and purpose in their repetitive coming and going.

A Limited Perspective

Even though the writer's perspective is limited, there are, I believe, valuable lessons to be learned in his series of comments on the times. He, of course, didn't foresee the scope of the power of God's redemptive purposes, and for that reason his comments aren't altogether satisfying to a reader of the prophets or of the New Testament. But what he implied here is still valid, even with the benefit of further discoveries in Scripture.

1. The Preacher was saying that God is far beyond the understanding of humankind. We cannot presume to see things from His level, but we must be content to trust Him for what we don't know or understand. After all, a God we could fully understand would be no God at all.
2. He also maintained that a realistic acceptance of our mortality helps us concentrate on using wisely the days and years that we do have. "So I saw that there is nothing better than that a man should rejoice in his work, for that is his lot. Who can bring him to see what will be after him?" (3:22, ESV).
3. Furthermore, these limitations of time and life impose upon human beings the necessity of trusting God (3:14), and that is their purpose.

The Consolations of Life (4:1–16)

As we move ahead now to this part of our scripture lesson, the Preacher takes us into a somewhat different area of thought. Up to this point he had concentrated on those realities that affected people in general. The cycle of time affects everyone the same way. The rich and the poor both die; the wise and the foolish both sink into futility. No one is exempted from the strain and pain of work, or from the psychological oppression of a world in which even our best words and greatest deeds make no difference.

Viewed from that perspective, we have a lot of company. If all effort, fortune, fame, talent come to the same end, then we are no worse or better off than a monarch of an oil-rich emirate, a world-class financier, the founder of a large social media outlet or a successful online store, or one of the country's favorite athletes. We are all caught in the cycle of repetitive events that end in death.

Next, however, the Preacher turns his attention to those things that make life futile because of the unfairness of conditions—the pain endured by some people, often without just cause—and not by others. Some people have a better life and a brighter future than others. It is this that causes us to question the meaning and purpose of life. We lash out against the seeming unfairness of it all.

Oppressors and the Oppressed

The Preacher begins this line of thought by saying that he "saw all the oppressions that are done under the sun" and while the oppressors had strength and power, the oppressed had no one to comfort or rescue them (4:1, ESV).

Perhaps every nation in the history of the world has taken advantage of the weaknesses—either in numbers or economically—of a certain segment of society. There has been oppression, conscious and unconscious, of minority groups—racial, social, and religious—as well as those in lower income brackets. In fact, there is a tendency to oppress or suppress most anyone who, one way or another, is different.

But there are always people like the Preacher whose conscience is touched because the oppressed "had no one to comfort them" (4:1, NASB). Yet we see the enormity of his feeling of hopelessness at that moment over the wrongs and the inequities, as he says it would be better for the oppressed if they had never been born (4:2–3). The seeming hopelessness of it all overwhelms him as he ponders the tormenting questions and doubts.

The Foolishness of Compulsive Striving

The Preacher next gives us several proverbs that have to do with the futility of a compulsive striving to outdo a neighbor (4:4–12). The tone is set in verse 4, "I have seen that every labor and every skill which is done is the result of rivalry between a person and his neighbor. This too is futility and striving after wind" (NASB). Our writer is speaking here of the deadliness of straining and striving in our work merely to do better than somebody else.

At the same time, he denounces the foolishly lazy person who is not productive (4:5). And by contrast he praises the person who leads a balanced life and who finds inspiration in moments of quiet reflectiveness (4:6). The point being made so far is that a stress-filled life of frantic effort for the sake of looking better and more prosperous than a neighbor produces nothing but emptiness and is like chasing after the wind.

The Preacher then focuses on the healthy value of cooperation as opposed to cutthroat competition (4:9–12): "Two are better than one," as most translations word the beginning of verse 9. We all need the support of one another. In the Christian sense, we draw strength, inspiration, and power from one another. To try to stand alone is to fall.

The Emptiness of Fame

In these closing verses of chapter 4 the Preacher speaks out against the foolishness and emptiness of striving to be famous (verses 13–16). He draws a vivid picture as he says it is far better to be an unknown and poor young man "than an old and foolish king" who refuses to take advice from anybody.

The comparisons in these verses are startling. The forces that drive people have not changed in 2,500 years and more. The headlines on our 24-hour news channels and the headlines of our papers and news sites are constant reminders of people in politics, in the professions, and in business whose dog-eat-dog attitude and obsession to have more and do more have positioned them in places of power and prominence. But then greed for material gain and power has corrupted their values and relationships until everything is lost, including reputation and self-respect.

The Preacher is right. Working and striving in a spirit of rivalry and destructive competition is hollow, empty, like trying to chase the wind. But a life of cooperation, of helping our neighbor across the street or across the world, is satisfying and worthwhile.

Father, help me to live a life of service—to You and to those around me. AMEN.

INSPIRATION FROM THE BOOK OF ECCLESIASTES

Vanity of vanities! All is vanity.

—Ecclesiastes 1:2 (ESV)

I've been feeling rather weighed down lately with family responsibilities, spending as much time as possible with a dying friend and coping with work deadlines. But tonight I remembered something I discovered several years ago, when I was feeling both burdened and somewhat depressed. I'd started reading Ecclesiastes, and it fit my mood so well that I just kept on until I'd finished the book (which is only eight short chapters). It was a healing catharsis for me then, and it had the same effect tonight. It's the deep honesty of the book that moves me so much. The writer puts into words all those vague, burdensome feelings most of us have at times, about the seeming futility of earthly life and its many injustices—feelings we're afraid to speak or even admit to ourselves.

Reading Ecclesiastes is like taking hold of both ends of a battery. It's a series of shocks that makes me want to commiserate, saying, "Yeah, that's the way I feel too!" Yet in the reading of it, I somehow come to a degree of acceptance of the alternating currents of life, knowing that all is in divine order, and that I can trust the great mystery of it all (see Ecclesiastes 3:11).

My experience of reading Ecclesiastes—the whole book from beginning to end—helped me emerge from the other end not dimmed out but glowing.

Thank You, Lord, for the Preacher's courageous honesty in writing the book of Ecclesiastes, and for its great truth that nothing matters but You.

—Marilyn Morgan King

To every thing there is a season, and a time to every purpose under the heaven.

—Ecclesiastes 3:1 (KJV)

"I've given up driving my car," my old friend said, "and, you know, it was one of the most difficult decisions I've ever had to make. We Americans love our cars and take them for granted as almost indispensable in our lives. When the time comes to hang up your keys, you feel a tremendous sense of loss, as if your life is severely limited. It left me with a real sense of depression."

"You seem to have gotten over that," I said. "How did you do it?"

"I turned to the Bible, as I often do with a problem, and found myself reading Ecclesiastes, where the Preacher says that there's a time for everything: 'A time to be born, and a time to die . . . a time to weep, and a time to laugh . . . a time to keep, and a time to cast away.' Those words are thousands of years old, but in their majestic cadences you can almost hear the clock of the universe tick. They made me think that even where driving a car is concerned, there is a time to stop, and a wise person must accept that necessity without feeling deprived or depressed. So that's what I've been trying to do."

"Good for you," I said, and hoped that someday I would be equally wise.

Father, grant me the wisdom to know when the time is right for hard decisions.

—*Arthur Gordon*

Notes

Notes

Notes

LESSON 5: ECCLESIASTES 5–10

Futility and Faith

Father, fill me up with Your faith! Help me to take on Your truth and reality—by faith—in spite of what others may say. AMEN.

In recent years sociologists as well as laypeople have begun to understand the importance of balance in our lives. Most advice revolves around work/life balance, but it goes beyond that. The desire to give a place to each part of our lives—such as our faith, our contributions to community, our health—is always a challenge. Despite its recent place in the spotlight, our struggle to find balance is not a modern phenomenon.

The writer of Ecclesiastes shows a concern for life that is out of balance, which in his thinking is a life that is affected by injustice, alienation, greed, dishonesty, and fear. The Ecclesiastes writer looks beyond the outward workings of a life that is out of balance to the roots and reasons for our imbalances. The world and our human nature cry out for justice, equity, meaning, and purpose, yet in the very nature of things, these needs do not find an answer.

In the section of the book of Ecclesiastes we will study now, we find the Preacher's complaints leveled against all areas of life. Everything seems to testify to the futility of the world. If there is an answer to all of this, it lies only with God. But humankind must do the best it can with a lower order of knowledge because people cannot penetrate the mystery that is God.

The Emptiness of Words (5:1–7)

The first and most notable way we attempt to set life right is with our language. This part of our scripture lesson may appear, at first, to be about worship, but actually its broader concern is the use of language, and the way the vanity or emptiness of life is increased and emphasized by our use of *many* words.

Words are to be guarded carefully, the Preacher says, otherwise they only contribute to the general senseless striving in life. Words are the source of much sin: we lie, cheat, and mislead, slander, debase, and condescend, with words. Worse yet, we pretend to worship with a great flood of pious words when our hearts are really not in it. The Preacher takes a dim view of a religion of words and more words, instructing the reader that "to listen is better than to offer the sacrifice of fools" (5:1, ESV). In fact, he bores right in when he says, "Be not rash with your mouth . . . let your words be few" (5:2–3, ESV).

We can only guess what the Preacher would think of our world in which millions of words—both spoken and written—spew out in scores of languages every minute over the internet, text messaging, and social media, as well as radio, TV, and print. Our floodlike outpouring of words would boggle his mind, but more than likely, his advice would be the same now as when he first spoke: Words must be used with caution and with justice.

When he speaks of the worship of God (in 5:1–2, 4, and 7), we come to the heart of what he wants us to hear. Karl Barth, one of the most widely appreciated theologians of the twentieth century, said that one of the gravest sins of humankind is self-justification. This leads us to ask, How and why do we use our words in worship? Is it to honor God? Or to parade before others our piety and devotion, our good intentions, and to justify ourselves? Here the Preacher makes it clear that if we talk too much, perhaps we should question our motives. Consequently, he says, "let your words be few" (5:2).

So often we feel the need to fill up the vacuum in our lives and in our relationships with words. This, according to the Preacher, is vanity and a striving after the wind.

Possession and Power (5:8–6:12)

The Preacher now turns his attention to the ways power and possessions add to the futility of life. His view of the abuse of power and the accompanying injustices is not at all what might be called "cynical." It stops short of cynicism because although the injustices he describes do occur, there is still a God who sees all these things and judges them (5:8).

Power creates a very seductive temptation. We fall into the trap of believing that we have power, that we can do anything without having to pay the consequences. But this is a subtle lie, for we do pay the consequences in the distortion of truth and blindness to our true responsibility.

Years ago Lord Acton warned against the corruption of power when he said, "Power tends to corrupt, and absolute power corrupts absolutely." Sensing this danger, the founding fathers of the United States felt the need to frame a Constitution that would limit power, deny the unwieldy growth of power in any one branch of government, and preserve powers for the states and the people. Most of our constitutional history centers upon the same distrust of power that the Preacher warns against in our scripture lesson.

The Mixed Blessing of Material Wealth

The Preacher moves now to a collection of sayings (5:9–19) that emphasize the truth that material wealth can be compared to a two-edged sword. He first makes it clear that material wealth is for the benefit of all and is needed by everyone—from the peasant who works the land to the king who rules it (5:9).

But on the other hand, he says those who possess great wealth may find little satisfaction in it (5:10–11), and it may cause concern and worry (5:12). In addition, there may be the possibility that a person who acquires and hoards wealth will be hurt somehow (5:13). Furthermore, there is the danger of losing wealth, and ultimately it *will* be lost when a person dies—then the fact that we had it at all will mean absolutely nothing (5:14–17).

Writer E. M. Forster wrote an essay titled "My Wood." In it he told about a small patch of wooded land that he used to enjoy. Whenever he walked through it and smelled the fragrance of the trees and flowers and watched the birds, he came away refreshed and revitalized.

Later Forster bought that parcel of wooded land. But then he had a very different experience. He was concerned whether the trees might become diseased, or whether his neighbor might encroach on his property. He couldn't sleep at night, he said, thinking that something or someone might violate his acreage.

As the Preacher says, it is a decided benefit to possess something of material value, but like all things in life, the benefits of ownership can unpredictably work against the one who labored to acquire it.

Some people can't stand to own a home. They worry over the possibility of a leaky roof or that the foundation may have a serious flaw or that the value of their property will depreciate. Such people stew over the thousand possibilities that accompany the ownership of property. The Preacher was aware of this in his time, and it colored his view of life's vanities.

The Enjoyment of Possessions

Time and again in the book of Ecclesiastes we have seen that the writer has contrasted one idea with another. First, there is the idea that a person longs for what is unattainable: knowledge of what is good and purposeful in a world that denies him that knowledge. He sees the world as a closed circle, beyond which he cannot penetrate. And because of this, he sees nothing but futility.

But besides this futility, we also discover one of the positive teachings of the book of Ecclesiastes: Even though we are denied what we long for by our own mortality and by the finitude of worldly existence, we can find something to receive with gratitude.

That is the idea the Preacher once again turns to as he reflects about possessions. Though they offer no ultimate solace in life, they are still, within those limits, good. They are from the hand of God and intended for our benefit (5:18–20).

The gnostic heresy that threatened to change the character of the early Christian church taught that matter was evil, and spirit, in contrast, was good. The church fathers fought this notion vigorously. Early Christians believed that the Bible clearly teaches that matter—whether the bodily flesh or material possessions—is not evil in and of itself. While some forms of matter may lead to evil, they are created and intended for good.

It is true that material possessions can become a cause for trouble and heartache, but only if we permit that to happen. While the Preacher warns against being trapped by greed and corruption, he also makes it clear that material possessions are God's gift to us, and we should receive them with thanksgiving—always remembering that we are to love the Giver more than the gift.

Wealth Doesn't Guarantee Enjoyment

As the Preacher moves into what we know as chapter 6, he continues to build on the ideas he has been discussing up to this point. Now he turns his attention to the fact that the possession of wealth doesn't necessarily bring personal enjoyment (6:1–12).

First, he tells us about a man who had amassed considerable wealth and who lived a life of honor, but he died without having an heir. This meant that he could no longer enjoy his wealth, and since he didn't have a child, there was no heir to enjoy it either. Then through some legal process someone, possibly a complete stranger, was assigned to be the heir, and apparently the assigned heir was a stranger who had no ties to the dead man. He didn't even provide a proper burial. Instead, he just went on to enjoy the dead man's wealth.

Now, a situation like this seems very strange to us, but the Preacher says that this sort of thing happened regularly in his culture. He has given us a prime example of a situation where neither the wealthy man nor his family could enjoy the full benefits of all that he had worked for and accumulated (6:1–2).

Next, in verses 3–5, our writer tells us about another man who was blessed with many children. He, too, had accumulated great wealth and lived a long life. On the surface it would appear that he had everything good going for him. But we're told that this man's life was filled with trouble and worry. And because of this, even though he had many heirs and lived a long life, he didn't enjoy his wealth at all. As a matter of fact, our writer says, "a stillborn child is better off" than he is (verse 3, ESV). That way he would have been spared a life full of trouble.

As the Preacher continues to ponder the dilemmas of life as he sees them, he seems to be asking, "What about those desires that cannot be filled or satisfied? Can it be that those things that give every indication of being a blessing do not, in fact, guarantee happiness or fulfillment?" (See 6:6–9).

All of these reflections of the Preacher help us to focus on an important principle: Happiness cannot be assured by either possessions or circumstances. Satisfaction with life comes only with a proper relationship to the God of life—not from the circumstances of life.

This is the great service that the book of Ecclesiastes provides for us. It causes us to reflect upon the futility of finding ultimate good within the closed circle of this world. If there is, indeed, a good to be found, then it must find its source elsewhere. We've seen that it is not in possessions or in long life. Even our family cannot provide it.

Wealth and possessions are good and to be enjoyed, but the moment they become our "gods"—that is, the moment we expect them to provide unfailing satisfaction with life—we ask of them more than they can give.

Guideposts for the Good Life (7:1–29)

In our scripture lesson now we are given several proverbs (7:1–14, 19–22). A reflection on personal experience appears in the middle of these (7:15–18), and chapter 7 ends with a reflection on the inadequacy of wisdom (7:23–29).

The first verse gives us a clue to the general line of reasoning that the Preacher is taking: "A good name is better than precious ointment; and the day of death than the day of one's birth" (7:1, KJV). This verse lauds the value of a good reputation. The idea being expressed here is that a good name—a good reputation and character—is of greater value than anything else we might possess.

Furthermore, the Preacher says, character is often gained by suffering loss, disappointment, and grief. Here is an important truth: When life is easy, we do not grow, and we do not mature in wisdom. So it is better to strive for those things that build character rather than those things that provide comfort and good times (7:14). Without difficulties we learn nothing. And without pain we do not grow.

The Snare of Injustice

An extension of this idea is that in trying to avoid pain ourselves, we often are willing to inflict it upon others. Plato raised this question when he asked which is better: to have injustice done to us or to avoid that prospect by doing what is unjust to someone else?

A man taught a class in a state penitentiary to inmates who were studying philosophy for college credit. When Plato's "which is better" question came up, one inmate answered it with, "Frankly, it's either me or them—and it's not going to be me!" As he read Plato, however, he gradually came around to accept—at least intellectually—a different point of view. Addressing this question in his famous dialogue *The Republic*, Plato insisted that it is better to find oneself the victim of injustice than to inflict it upon others.

Plato's reasoning is much like the Preacher's: If we endure pain, suffering, and injustice, our character will gain from it. But if we inflict harm on others, even though we may gain temporarily, we unfailingly lose what is most essential to our happiness: the ability to live well.

Jesus made a similar point when He taught, "What good will it be for someone to gain the whole world, yet forfeit their soul?" (Matthew 16:26, NIV). What we gain through injustice we lose in a genuine ability to enjoy what we have.

The Preacher also takes us in this direction when he writes, "For oppression makes a wise person look foolish, and a bribe corrupts the heart" (7:7, NASB). For similar reasons we must avoid those things that cause us to act unjustly. Our writer then includes proverbs that speak against impatience and pride (7:8), anger (7:9), and resentment over change (7:10).

We see in all of this that the Preacher has a firm grasp on the idea that evil is any thing or any circumstance that causes us to trust in *it* rather than in God. This is vividly illustrated in verses 11 to 14 of chapter 7. Here he wants us to see that the good has this striking quality: Whether it *seems* good or evil, it teaches us to trust in God alone.

Though John might well have, at first, thought of his imprisonment on the island of Patmos to be a dreadful hardship, the vision that he experienced there must have made it all worthwhile. The immortal *Pilgrim's Progress* was the good that came out of John Bunyan's experience in jail. And Aleksandr Solzhenitsyn, at the end of his many hard years in the Soviet prison, said, "Thank you, Prison!" because it brought him an insight into a rich and full life.

Living with Life's Inequities

Next, the Preacher looks into himself and shares certain things he has observed (7:15–18). His observations here don't come as a surprise, for we've all seen evil people who give every indication of living long and prosperous lives while good people can suffer and die young. This is part of the futility of life as the Preacher sees it.

How often have we asked why when a child or a teenager or a young parent was killed in an accident or was a victim of a tragic illness? The entire book of Job is devoted to this question.

As we work our way through this book of Ecclesiastes and get to know the Preacher, we cannot help but be impressed and grateful for his honesty in asking the questions, even though he frequently offers us unwelcome and depressing views of the way he sees things. He's helpful, though, in somewhat of a negative way because he shows us where the blind alleys are.

That is what the book of Ecclesiastes does for us: It warns us against false or wrong turns, especially the ones that *appear* to be right.

Among those wrong turns are those the Preacher mentions here. False religiosity, with scrupulous attention to the law (7:16), is a wrong way. But just as bad is the opposite—a cynical flouting of the law (7:17). Now, however, our writer points us to the right way: "It is good that you grasp one thing while not letting go of the other; for one who fears God comes out with both of them" (7:18, NASB).

Just as we found in the book of Proverbs, the fear of God—awe and reverence for God—is the true guidepost for the good life. This way avoids the fanaticism of either religious presumption or rebellion against the law.

Wisdom Has Its Limits

The Preacher concludes this group of proverbs with sayings that are focused on two major thoughts (7:19–29).

The first is that wisdom is good, but it is powerless against the profound mystery of life (7:19, 23–28). There is the mystery of what is right and good, and this is impossible to know satisfactorily. One of the early heresies of the church claimed to have special knowledge that gave them power in the face of life's difficulties. The followers of this heresy were known as Gnostics—from the Greek word for "knowledge." This idea of having "special knowledge" or insight has been a destructive force in the church down through the centuries. Inevitably, the claim of possessing special knowledge fuels the fires of pride and fanaticism.

Once again, the important contribution of the Preacher is that he often puts matters into proper perspective. He claims there is much good in knowledge and wisdom. But he refrains from claiming too much. His real wisdom lies in moderation and humility.

A well-known educator was speaking to a group of teachers. He made a point that must ring true with anyone who has seriously tried to learn or to teach. "We don't begin to learn," he said, "until we are willing to admit ignorance." Those whose pride prevents them from admitting what they do not know have a difficult time learning. The teacher, therefore, must make it safe for a student to admit what he or she doesn't know.

The Preacher raises this educational principle to a philosophic art. It follows in the train of other things he has been saying. If the fear of God is necessary to build wisdom, then humility before the One who can teach us—God Himself—is the starting point of our learning from Him.

Everyone Fails Sometime

The second idea that these verses revolve around is that doing wrong is universal. Moral failure does not belong to the few, or even to the many, but to everyone. The Preacher calls attention to this ever-present reality (7:20–22, 29).

The fact that wrongdoing—and the guilt that results—is a problem found in every human life is more than just a bit of information for our writer. Even less is it a way of justifying moral evil. We might respond to our own moral failures by saying, "Oh well, nobody's perfect." But that is not the point the Preacher is making.

Instead, he is saying just the opposite. Rather than saying that since everyone is wrong, I am okay, he instead says that since everyone is wrong, that includes me too. The point is that no one can justify himself. Everyone has taken the wrong route and lives in rebellion against God. In writing to the Christians at Rome, Paul said, "For all have sinned, and come short of the glory of God" (Romans 3:23, KJV).

But this also leads us to another important realization. When we say, "Everyone does what is wrong and that *includes* me," it also means that we can be more tolerant and understanding of others. The limits of wisdom, and the limits of our powers to live a moral life, do not permit us to judge harshly (see especially 7:21–22). Quite to the contrary, the evil we find around us should cause us to reflect seriously on the evil we find within us.

The Rewards of Wisdom (8:1–15)

Do you recall now the tone of the writing at the beginning of the book of Ecclesiastes? But now the tone has changed considerably. At the beginning it seemed that the Preacher could hardly have made a stronger case against the world as we find it; it was a dismal account of things with little room for hope. You might call that short section the first movement, as in a work of classical music, stating the theme that will carry throughout.

What could be called the second movement in the book of Ecclesiastes begins with the "seasons and times" poem in chapter 3. This new movement continues the criticism and doubt, asking if there could ever be found any meaning or purpose in life, and then doubting that there could be. But along with this new movement, we begin to catch just a glimmer of light. We begin to see that perhaps we can find some good in receiving what God does give us. Though our prospects are limited, we must accept those limits.

Now, however, as we move into chapter 8, we see more and more implications—positive religious implications—coming from that little glimmer of hope that tells us there might be some good in all of this after all.

These proverbs in this part of our scripture lesson testify to the fact that even with the Preacher's rather limited view of life—even with his small amount of faith in God—positive results can come about.

We see here that wisdom (8:1–9) includes both submission to authorities such as the king and humility because of our lack of knowledge about the future. And we see that even the king must show humility as he acknowledges a truth that is above and beyond him.

In Jewish tradition one of the chief virtues of Moses was humility. Because he claimed little for himself and submitted his will to God's will, he was found worthy as the great prophet, priest, and leader of Israel.

Humility is the willingness to receive, even with gratitude, the life we have been given. It is humility, more than any other virtue, that makes us fit for service to God.

Jesus also taught humility. He did so by willingly receiving His destiny on the Cross, by assuming the way of a servant, and by rejecting the role of political power. He taught His disciples not to lord it over one another as the Gentile rulers did but to be servants.

A title of honor in the early church was *diakonos*—a deacon, or, literally, a servant. Paul called himself a *doulos,* a bond servant or a slave for Christ (see Romans 1:1). Humility is always the true touchstone of spiritual greatness in the Christian life. Without genuine humility we do not glorify Christ.

So the Preacher—as limited as his view of human wisdom might have been—touched upon something wonderfully important in the life of faith. And it comes out in many variations in this part of our lesson. But all of these variations focus on the truth that what is good in life is found not out of a desire for what we do not have but in our gratitude for what we already have been given.

The Problem of the Wicked Who Succeed

Next, the Preacher returns to a problem that is close to the heart of all his writing (8:10–17): Why do those who do wrong, and perpetrate injustices, often seem to get away with their evil deeds? But not only do they escape unpunished, they even prosper. How does this square with a world that is supposed to be governed by law and justice?

The Preacher is confident that sooner or later justice is served. But he still wrestles with the senselessness of existence that we encountered before in his writing when we see that justice has not yet been served. "There is something else meaningless that occurs on earth: the righteous who get what the wicked deserve, and the wicked who get what the righteous deserve. This too, I say, is meaningless" (8:14, NIV).

The answer to these problems, however, is assigned to the mystery of God (8:16–17). The answer cannot be known. For this reason we do well to act and think with humility.

In verse 15 we find an often-paraphrased statement, "A man hath no better thing under the sun, than to eat, and to drink, and to be merry" (KJV). This is often quoted as if it were advice or license to follow a hedonistic and pleasure-seeking way of life. But that is not the Preacher's meaning here.

Instead, he is recommending the enjoyment of life's simple pleasures. Rather than strive for what belongs only to God (that is, the kind of knowledge that answers all questions), we are to be content with what we have. To enjoy it is to respond to what God has done. It is to be thankful. Once again we see that the quality of life that is most treasured in the book of Ecclesiastes is humility. And the character of that life is one of receiving, and acknowledging with thanks, what we have already been given.

A Place for Hope (9:1–18)

As we move along with the Preacher's proverbs in Ecclesiastes, we can give a sigh of relief to be free from the gravity of those early chapters. It seemed as if the condition of life that he outlined for us, at first, would leave room for only despair or cynicism. Yet through it all, he continued to refer to the mystery and power of God. These were subtle hints that the tone of his comments would change.

It is true in this part of our lesson now (9:1–10) that the outcome might still seem to fall short of the hope and joy we know as believers today. But we do find in these verses a genuine trust in God and a place for hope.

Hope, in fact, is the focus of these verses. It is evident, as we have already seen, that the Preacher believed that death was the end of everything. This was the prevailing thought in Judaism in those times. We see here, though, that within the limits of life as he knew it there is hope: "For whoever is joined to all the living, there is hope; for better a live dog, than a dead lion" (9:4, NASB).

The idea behind this verse is sometimes paraphrased as "Where there's life, there's hope." Hope is an essential quality in life. Jürgen Moltmann, a German theologian, was drafted as a young teenager into Hitler's army during World War II. He was soon captured and sent to a prisoner-of-war camp in Belgium. Later he was imprisoned in England and Scotland. With the end of the war and the defeat of the Nazi regime, word reached the German prisoners that many of their beautiful cities had been reduced to rubble. Next they heard that the Nazis were responsible for horrible atrocities in their concentration camps. Dr. Moltmann said that when his fellow prisoners heard those stories, many of them lost hope. In their despair, some of them died; they could not live without hope.

Dr. Moltmann was able to endure the crisis, he thought, because an American chaplain had given him a copy of the New Testament with the Psalms. There, especially in the Psalms, he read of men in hopeless circumstances who put their trust in God. Because of that initial experience with these hope-filled Scriptures, Moltmann went back to Germany and decided to study theology.

He wanted to learn more about that hope that had saved him so he could help his fellow countrymen to find redemption and a new life in the midst of their post-war devastation.

Later he wrote his well-known book, *Theology of Hope*. Through this he was able to share the biblical understanding of hope. God, Moltmann showed, reveals Himself to us by giving us hope.

Strengthened by Joy

The Preacher shifts now from "hope" to "joy" (9:7–10). Here we find an assurance that we can live our lives in the knowledge that God has accepted us (9:7). And knowing that we are received and approved by God can mean that we live with joy.

Joy, of course, generally has a meaning that is distinct from happiness. Happiness may depend upon our circumstances in life. But joy is a disposition that allows us to feel that we are equal to life no matter what the circumstances may be. Joy is an inner sense of strength closely related to hope. If we feel that we can meet the new day with abundant resources of confidence and emotional strength, then we can say we have joy. If we feel defeated even before we begin, then we lack joy.

The Role of Chance

The concluding verses of this chapter (9:11–18) find the Preacher once again turning back to his cautious habit of saying that "nothing is certain." Even if we have wisdom, it may not bring us honor. This idea is illuminated in verses 13–16.

No human virtue guarantees success or good fortune. The Preacher says, "Again I saw that under the sun the race is not to the swift, nor the battle to the strong, nor bread to the wise, nor riches to the intelligent, nor favor to those with knowledge, but time and chance happen to them all" (9:11, ESV). This line of thought could easily turn to fatalism—the notion that all things are determined by outside forces over which we have no control. But remember that the central thought in the book of Ecclesiastes is not the uselessness of our human powers but their limits.

Humility, which comes from an awareness of our limits, is different from a cynical resignation in the face of hopelessness and disappointment. No, our writer is not preaching fatalism, but, as before, he will not claim more than his observations warrant. In the final analysis, we are driven to the conclusion that all hope must be invested in God.

Contrasts in Wisdom and Folly (10:1–20)

Proverbs such as the ones we find here help us to think about issues from different angles. They evoke images, and for that reason they lodge themselves in our imagination and continue to work upon our thoughts. They are like medicine contained in a time-release capsule—the effects continue to last as long as the images return to our thoughts.

We easily picture, for instance, the flies in the ointment (10:1, KJV), "servants upon horses, and princes walking as servants" (10:7, KJV), or the man digging a pit who falls into his own pit (10:8). The pictures have messages, but the messages are all the more remembered because of the pictures.

In this part of our scripture lesson we have a variety of proverbs that give us vivid contrasts between wisdom and folly. One image that gives us the sense of the Preacher's thought is in this proverb: "A wise man's heart is at his right hand; but a fool's heart at his left" (10:2, KJV). The right represents righteousness and the left signifies evil.

Wisdom, as we see in these proverbs, is not especially or exclusively an intellectual quality. More than anything it is a quality of the entire character of a person. It is not only the way a person thinks but what a person does, and what a person does habitually. We think of the intellect as a potential quality in a person's life, an ability to do something. But wisdom, for the Wisdom writer, is not simply a potential for doing something; it is what we actually do.

Incarnational Thinking: Wisdom and Action

Authentic wisdom proves itself in practice—that is the ancient Hebrew understanding of wisdom. By contrast, our generation and culture tend to be more abstract. We judge a person by test scores, vocational interests, good intentions, and so on. We might do well to incorporate a Hebrew sense of realism.

For a century or more the state of Missouri has been known as the "show me" state. As people moved west and settled in the farming regions along the Mississippi and Missouri Rivers, they professed not to be interested in whether a person made a good talk but only whether that person did what he said he would do. Our witness for Christ and our devotion to God is ultimately demonstrated in how we live. That kind of realism and wisdom could well be called "incarnational theology"—not abstract ideas about God but a living demonstration of who He is.

Father, give me a knowledge of Your ways as You give me a desire to do Your will. AMEN.

When times are good, be happy; but when times are bad, consider this: God has made the one as well as the other.

—Ecclesiastes 7:14 (NIV)

I was chatting with a friend the other day about the last few difficult years and the toll they have taken. "I wish we had a time machine," she said, "so things could go back to the way they were."

There are days when I wish that, too, but time moves in one direction and one direction only. The one force that exists outside the bounds of time is God. He connects the past to the present to the future because He exists everywhere.

I think as we move through time, we move closer to God. Time is our path to Him, our spiritual trajectory. I don't know how many times I've wished I could go back and fix the mistakes I've made or relive the difficult times in my life with more wisdom and faith. And maybe those times were difficult precisely because I lacked sufficient faith. Yet those were also the times when I learned and grew. My faith was made stronger even when I doubted it, even when I resisted. And I have resisted God's will as often as I have accepted it.

I felt bad for my friend, so I said, "We do have a time machine. We're in it right now; we just can't go backward, only forward. There's no reverse gear!"

That got a smile out of her, and we both felt a little better about these past few years, realizing that the temporal breeze was in our hair.

Lord, You are with us always, past, present, and future. I pray my faith grows as I move closer to You.

—*Edward Grinnan*

Notes

Notes

Notes

LESSON 6: ECCLESIASTES 11–12

Wisdom for Young and Old

Lord, help me to incline my heart to wisdom, understanding, discernment; to be able to comprehend the good from the bad, the best from the good. AMEN.

Today there are numerous popular websites and apps, thousands of books, television and radio programs, newspaper columns—and in fact a whole industry—dedicated to giving advice on how to earn, save, and invest money. People know that the resources they have may be put to good use and bring profit. Or they may easily and sometimes quickly be squandered, and the result can be financial ruin. Investing, put simply, involves knowing where to place our money, and when.

The Preacher focuses now on the most important of all investments—that of human life. He finds that the human knowledge of what is true and good is limited. It does involve, at the least, knowing what to do and how to handle what God has given us. It is important to use time well and to avoid laziness. We are also advised not to act or speak out of inordinate pride. The only prudent course for any of us, because of the uncertainty of events, is to acknowledge that we are in God's hands—our lives are invested in Him. But there's more; we are also on the receiving end of things. God has invested in us; He has given us *time* and *material possessions*.

Our scripture lesson now directs our attention to these gifts—our use of time, the fleeting years of life, and the insecurity of our material possessions. In order to anchor our lives to what is truly important and dependable, we, along with the Preacher, need to take a long, serious look at these gifts from God and how we handle them.

Work, Investment, and the Mystery of Life (11:1-6)

Over and over again, our writer has expressed his belief that since we can't know the future, we should concentrate on the current events of our daily lives. However, it isn't his intention to let us off the hook when it comes to planning and being willing to undertake the usual risks necessary to life.

Risk-Taking Faith

The opening words of the scripture passages for our lesson, "Cast thy bread upon the waters: for thou shalt find it after many days" (11:1, KJV), are familiar to many people, and the verse is often understood as a proverb related to the idea that if we act wisely and favorably toward others, they will respond the same way toward us. However, the reference is more likely to the wisdom of sending a grain crop to a foreign port in order to receive a good return on an investment. The translation of this verse in the New International Version, for example, reflects that interpretation: "Ship your grain across the sea; after many days you may receive a return."

In addition, we can look at these verses as more than just investment counsel. Imagine, if you can, what it meant in the ancient Mediterranean world to load a year's crop of grain on a sailing ship and send it to a distant port. The risk was high. There was always danger that a killer storm would drive the ship onto a rocky coastline and it would sink, or that marauding pirates would confiscate the cargo, or that unscrupulous agents would cheat the seller and the buyer alike. Insurance against such possibilities didn't exist. There were no guarantees. But for the sake of a more profitable market, grain sellers and farmers were lured into sending their products "over the waters."

The proverb that the Preacher gives us here urges his readers of all time to be willing to take reasonable risks. The greatest opportunities inevitably involve a risk. A proverb in our own language states it well: "Nothing ventured, nothing gained." Without an element of risk we lose out on much that gives life its inner motivation.

So the book of Ecclesiastes naturally includes this idea within its theme. The Preacher has said, as we have seen, that life cannot be fully understood; it is hedged in by mystery that we cannot unravel. What is left for the human being, however, is not to act out of pride *when* we do not have the answers or to resign in despair *because* we do not have the answers. The answer is neither pride nor despair, but it is an acknowledging of our limits and a trusting of ourselves to the mystery of life. In other words, the approach to a life of risks and dangers and unanswerable questions is humility and faith.

So the advice to "cast your bread upon the waters" applies to all of life. The writer is saying, "Take the risk—just as you watch your ship loaded with a full season's labors sail out of the harbor to unknown ports, trust your life to the unknown mystery of God."

Life is necessarily a risk, but the risk is also an opportunity. The fear of risks and the fear of a crisis can become more than sensible caution; it can turn into a fear of life. It is no wonder that the biblical use of the term "faith" is often discussed in contrast to the idea of fear, as in "faith over fear." It was not doubt that the prophets of the Old Testament spoke out against; they spoke against the timid and fearful distrust of God's promises and the cowardly failure to act upon them. It is a theme that appears many times in the Old Testament.

Living with the Unpredictable Element in Life

Still speaking of investments, our writer now urges caution (11:2). Don't count on only one or two transactions, but divide it among several plans (11:2), because you don't know what might happen. Another way to put it is simply, "Don't put all your eggs in one basket."

The Preacher follows up this caution in verse 3 by saying that things inevitably happen: A full cloud will bring rain, and a tree, at the right time, will fall, and we cannot undo what is done. He implies, therefore, that we must prepare for the inevitable. People take out health and life insurance, not because they anticipate illness and death, but precisely because they cannot anticipate it. Wise foresight is the best course. Wisdom always keeps in view the unpredictability of life.

The Ecclesiastes writer helps us to keep these matters in balance. Prudence—taking measures against an unpredictable future—is not lack of faith. It is, in fact, a measure of humility, which is a primary ingredient in faith.

Caution! Not Fear

We are accustomed to thinking that virtues and vices are opposites—qualities or actions that are poles apart. But, in fact, what makes our own sin difficult to diagnose is that it is often prompted by our virtues—good qualities that we separate from the context of real life.

For example, a brave person exercises courage in being a thief. A man of much human sympathy becomes unfaithful to his wife when he is prompted by sympathy for another woman. A person who exercises self-control becomes unsympathetic to those who are weaker, and his very ability to control his emotions makes him capable of cruelty. A woman is thrifty in her use of money; she possesses a virtue that easily turns into stinginess.

As we have seen, the Preacher speaks favorably of a cautious, prudent, and wise approach to life—always taking into consideration the element of unpredictability. But even this virtue—a kind of wise foresight—can shade over into an unhealthy fear of life. While we want to keep from foolishly ignoring dangers, we can all too easily fall into the trap of failing to take any action at all. "He who watches the wind [waiting for all conditions to be perfect] will not sow [seed], and he who looks at the clouds will not reap [a harvest]" (11:4, AMP). Caution may keep us from rushing headlong into danger, but fear paralyzes us. Foolhardiness and fear alike work against the best course in a full and purposeful life.

Positive Living in an Unpredictable World

In much of life we see that the preferred course is the middle way. Be cautious, but do not fear. Be industrious, but do not worship work. Enjoy what you have, but know that it does not last. Love all that you are given—but not too much. After all, everything vanishes sooner or later.

Next, we come to the Preacher's most typical kind of counsel (11:5–6). Since we don't know ahead of time the results of our efforts, we are to work prudently and wisely. It is in positive work and positive action that we exercise faith. The work of faith recognizes that nothing can be counted on ultimately except God. But it also refuses to be paralyzed into inaction by fear of loss.

There is a tempered optimism in this attitude, because the Preacher also recognizes that something good *can* happen, "for you do not know which will succeed, whether this or that, or whether both will do equally well" (11:6, NIV). The writer is unwilling to predict good, but he is open to the possibility of good things happening. The Preacher's tempered optimism can be described as "Prepare for the worst and hope for the best."

Life Is Sweet, but Short (11:7–10)

The theme of the book of Ecclesiastes continues as our writer speaks of the brevity of life. He doesn't deny that the days of childhood and youth hold attractions and blessings that we would want to keep—but they do not last. Neither does the Preacher deny the possibility of a long life—full to the brim with many blessings (11:7–8). But even so, the "days of darkness," or the days beyond this life "under the sun," are of an even greater number.

But the Preacher now carries this point further. He speaks of the goodness of youth—but also of the fact that it is short-lived (11:9–10). When we are young, we can really only look ahead and see the possibility of what seems like an endless stream of days. And then one day, without warning, we take stock of our lives and realize that more than likely, there are more days behind us than before us. It is no wonder that the early rabbis speculated that Ecclesiastes was written in Solomon's old age. Age gives us a certain clarity about many things. And one of these is that our young years are brief.

If the heart of education is learning what lasts and what does not, then our writer has done us a service by focusing on the all-important reality that human life is limited or framed by time. His message is unrelenting: All things pass away, all things vanish like a vapor, they are a "vanity of vanities"— emptiness. He forces us to the very practical conclusion that, apart from God Himself, we can put our ultimate trust in nothing.

The Wisdom of Youth: Remembering the Creator (12:1–8)

We come now to several verses that are somber in tone and weighty in their serious approach to mortality, yet they make up one of the most beautiful poems found in any language. "Remember your Creator in the days of your youth," the writer counsels (12:1, NIV). The words are sharp and full of power—especially after we have followed the Preacher through all that has gone before and have reflected that all created things come to an end.

So, "How should we start out?" the writer asks, in effect. We naturally seek to anchor our lives in wisdom or wealth or secure ourselves with pleasure or work. One by one we have seen these substantial treasures in life wither and die under the writer's overpowering realism. Nothing lasts. Everything is limited. All is vanity—empty and worthless in the final analysis.

A Picture of Old Age

Next follows a poignant picture of the failing years of old age (12:2–7). First, the vision dims (12:2). Then the arms and legs ("keepers of the house") tremble, deprived of their former strength. The old are bent low with age, and teeth ("grinders") are missing (12:3). The imagery continues as it speaks of dulled hearing and sleep that is disturbed by the chirping of a bird (12:4). Fear of falling and fear of travel are descriptive of the feeble and aged (12:5). The "almond tree" that flowers hints at hair as white as the almond blossom, and the old are pictured dragging themselves along as they walk like the grasshopper, and "[sexual] desire shall fail" (12:5, KJV). All this happens as death awaits and while the professional mourners mill about the street, waiting for the inevitable funeral procession so they can be paid for their loud mourning (12:5).

All of these images in verses 5 and 6 suggest the fragility of life—and the ruin that is left of life when it ends. The poem evokes strange feelings of the abandonment and isolation of death.

The Stark Reality of Life

At the same time, the poem expresses the Preacher's argument in the strongest terms. Think carefully, it says to us, about that which does not last. For if you look for something on which to anchor your existence, you will not find it in this life. The Preacher's constant "vanity of vanities" has done its job. If we have listened to him and seen the images that he has cast up to fuel our imaginations, then we have seen life in its starkest reality. And we will know, as he intends for us to know, that for the greatest good—and the only lasting value—we must look beyond the things of this life.

Everything gives way to time. Life itself ends, and the spirit or breath returns to God who gave it (12:7). No other book in our Bible paints this picture so graphically. Now the recurring theme surfaces again: "Vanity of vanities, saith the preacher; all is vanity" (12:8, KJV). Everything is empty. Nothing remains. All wisdom, wealth, effort, and even the material evidence of life itself are like a vapor—they disappear, and nothing is left of them.

But the *apparent* theme, as we have seen, only sets in relief the true perspective of the Preacher. He addresses all of his observations in light of the reality of God. And he counsels humility, not because humanity is nothing, but because God is great. The vanity and emptiness of human effort is seen in light of the overwhelming power of a created world that is governed by a God who sets times and seasons.

The vanity and meaninglessness of the world is seen in contrast to God, and apart from God. Throughout the book of

Ecclesiastes we are invited to see that if there is any meaning or reward in life, it has to do with the majesty of God.

Epilogue: The Whole Duty (12:9–14)

These last verses of the book of Ecclesiastes do three things. First, they commend the teachings of the sage or the wise man (12:9–11). Second, they caution the young man against excessive study of too many books (12:12). And, third and final, they summarize the positive element in the Preacher's teaching (12:13–14). Let's look at each of these three parts of the epilogue.

The Teachings

The skill of the Preacher has much to do with the fact that he is an effective teacher. He took much care to find the right words, and to arrange the proverbs in a proper order (12:9–10). Moreover, he wrote "words of truth" (12:10, KJV). All of these add what we would call *rhetoric*.

There is a great need for this skill. For the truth remains hidden if it cannot be stated well, attractively, and clearly. Truth must be expressed in a way that motivates. "The words of the wise are [sharp] like goads" (12:11, ESV), our writer says. In addition, these teachings must be memorable. They must stay in the mind "like firmly embedded nails" (12:11, NIV). Our writer—the Preacher—was a master at using words in a convincing way.

It is necessary to not only speak the truth but to say it clearly and in plain language. The Preacher has done this so well that he even speaks to us over the time chasm of more than two thousand years—and in picture language we can still understand.

Of Too Much Study

It may seem strange that in a writing of this kind we find a warning against books and study. But we do: "Of making many books there is no end; and much study is a weariness of the flesh" (12:12, KJV).

The writer was probably referring to something rather specific that his first readers would have readily understood. Some students of Ecclesiastes have suggested that he was warning against the great influx of foreign books and foreign philosophies. It would hardly seem characteristic of a Hebrew writer to counsel restraint in study—since, of all people, those who produced and preserved the Old Testament were noted for concentrating on study.

One thing, however, we do know. That is, the Old Testament writers always tended to see the real object of learning as consisting of practical results in behavior. You might remember that, as we studied the book of Proverbs, wisdom was never seen as abstract ideas but always as concrete principles we could put into practice. Orthodoxy (right teaching) always was judged by *orthopraxy* (right practice).

So the Wisdom writer might well have warned against study that didn't result in right behavior. Remember that he saw wisdom itself—along with knowledge—as limited, and in terms of life's ultimate questions, it was futile. In view of its futility he warned against burning ourselves out on various kinds of speculation that do not change behavior and strengthen life.

Life's Essentials

As we look at the last two verses of our scripture lesson, we see one solid positive note. We will not be surprised at the words because they are implied in so much of what has gone before. This, however, is the "conclusion, when everything has been heard . . . fear God and keep His commandments, because this applies to every person" (12:13, NASB). Indeed, this is the fundamental nature and quality of wisdom.

Now we see that, after all, something remains that *is* good and *will* last. It is our obedience to God (12:13), even though every good work will be revealed only as God Himself brings it out into the open (12:14). Charles Spurgeon put it well when he said, "Faith and obedience are bound up in the same bundle. He that obeys God, trusts God; and he that trusts God, obeys God."

Most certainly, these closing comments of the Preacher give us an encouraging and enlightening word. In our weakness and shortsightedness we try to find safety and strength and purpose in what we possess—wealth, wisdom, reputation, and the ability to work. But the wisdom of the book of Ecclesiastes has shown us that what lasts and is reliable is who and what we have become.

In his way, the Preacher in the book of Ecclesiastes forces us to probe the deep realities of life until we come to see them in a new way. We confront the reality that life isn't worthwhile and of value because of the possessions or pleasure or power we gain. Instead we come to see that it is in *being* and *doing* as an outgrowth of obedience to God that gives life richness, meaning, and purpose.

Being and *doing* in obedience to God is not some passive or empty thing that, to use the words of the Preacher, is "vanity of vanities." Rather, *being* and *doing* is the faithful volunteer who helps provide meals at a soup kitchen. It is the Sunday school teacher who toils and prepares every week to teach young children about God's love. It is the church member who visits or sends cards of encouragement to the ill or lonely. It is any man or woman of God who empties self in authentic concern for people in need.

In the final analysis, it is the act of doing something well for God.

Almighty God, help me to not just do the works of righteousness but to be a work of righteousness; and help me to not just be a work of righteousness but to do the works of righteousness. Amen.

A CLOSER LOOK AT ECCLESIASTES

The book of Ecclesiastes, like so much of the Bible, has imprinted itself upon society for generations. Often without being aware that we are doing so, we quote from the eminently quotable ponderings of the Preacher. Here are some common expressions derived from Ecclesiastes that have made their way into our everyday vernacular.

- **There is nothing new under the sun.** We tend to draw on this phrase, which occurs early in the book of Ecclesiastes—chapter 1, verse 9—when we feel cynical about the possibility that change can occur or when we are trying to create or do something new and discover that someone has done the same thing already. Shakespeare likely borrowed from this verse for the opening line of his Sonnet 59: "If there be nothing new but that which is hath done before, how are our brains beguil'd."
- **Eat, drink, and be merry.** Often used as an excuse to overindulge, this expression is loosely quoted from Ecclesiastes 8:15, and others throughout history

have borrowed and reshaped it. The ancient Greek philosopher Epicurus wrote, "Eat, drink, and be merry, for tomorrow we die." We hear echoes of the Preacher's words in Jesus's statement from one of His parables: "And I will say to myself, 'You have many goods stored up for many years to come; relax, eat, drink, and enjoy yourself!'" (Luke 12:19, NASB). And later the Apostle Paul paraphrased it when he wrote in his first letter to the Corinthians about the Resurrection: "If the dead are not raised, let's eat and drink, for tomorrow we die" (15:32, NASB).

- **A fly in the ointment.** This vivid word picture means that a small flaw or irritant can ruin something that is otherwise good. A similar expression is "One bad apple spoils the whole bunch." While this expression is not an exact quote from the Bible, its origins are clear when we read, "Dead flies cause the ointment of the apothecary to send forth a stinking savour" (Ecclesiastes 10:1, KJV).

- **Vanity of vanities, all is vanity.** While not perhaps as commonly spoken, this idiom quotes from Ecclesiastes 1:2. This or variants of this wording are used in much the same way today as when the words were written thousands of years ago. We might use this expression when we feel discouraged or disheartened. We worry our best efforts yield nothing, that there is little meaning or value in life, that nothing really matters. More humorously, we might say this about or to someone we know who seems overly preoccupied (another meaning of the word *vain*) about their appearance or reputation.

  The book of Ecclesiastes resonates with us because its thoughts, questions, and conclusions are part of the very fabric of human nature—the struggle to understand our purpose, the meaning of life, the value of the things we do and say—which is the same today as when Ecclesiastes was written.

Notes

Notes

Notes

LESSON 7: SONG OF SONGS 1–3

The Lover and the Beloved

Almighty God, I am overwhelmed by the love You have toward me. Thank You for drenching me daily in Your love. AMEN.

The Title (1:1)

When we say that something is the best or the greatest of its kind, we might use an expression such as "the day of all days," or "the game of games." Hebrew-speaking people passed on that expression to us. Our forefathers had read in the Bible (translated from the mostly Hebrew Old Testament) of God as the "God of gods and LORD of lords" (Deuteronomy 10:17), and of the Babylonian king Nebuchadrezzar as a "king of kings" (Ezekiel 26:7). The special place in the Temple was called the Holy of Holies.

They also knew of the Song of Songs, a title that meant to the Israelite people that this was the greatest of all songs. Imagine that today—if out of all the songs written and sung and recorded, we were to agree that one stood above all the rest as the best of songs. That would be an extravagant claim for any work of art. But that precisely is the claim made in the very title of these eight chapters of a love song.

Its Place in the Bible

The question posed most frequently about this song, however, is not why it makes such an extravagant claim for itself. If we read this book through, taking it very literally, we see immediately that this is a love song—or several love songs pulled together—about a rustic young woman and a king who is her lover and husband. Such being the case, we might well ask, "Why is this book in the Bible at all?"

Even if this is the greatest love song of all times, why would a poem about love between a man and a woman be included in the list of biblical books that we call the sacred canon, the authoritative list of books generally accepted as the inspired Word of God? It is characteristic of our times to draw sharp distinctions between what we might classify religious as compared to a nonreligious or secular subject like romantic love. The connection between romance, love, and marriage, on the one hand, and the language of worship was, however, not far-fetched to the ancient Jews and for Christians of the Middle Ages.

To the Jews of the first century and before, this love song held within it a great mystery. Outwardly it appeared to be only a love song, but inwardly it conveyed the idea of God's love of Israel.

Because the language of God's love is conveyed so strongly in the language of human love, a frequent saying—often cited by church fathers—was that Jews under the age of 30 were not to read and study this portion of scripture. The restriction was applied, not because the language was so sensual, but because the mystery was considered so potent and deep that it was likely, they thought, to be misconstrued by immature minds.

The Targums, an Aramaic translation of the Hebrew Scriptures, paraphrased the song to make it an allegory of Israel's escape from Egypt. For this reason the Song was included among the five festal scrolls and was read on the eighth day of the feast of Passover. In other interpretative literature on the Hebrew Scriptures this book is called "the most praiseworthy, most excellent, most highly treasured among the songs."

This high place that the Song occupies was not lost in the early church. Christians viewed it as an allegory of Christ's love and betrothal to the church. The venerable third-century church father Origen wrote twelve volumes exploring its mysteries. Bernard of Clairvaux, the great twelfth-century saint, delivered eighty-six sermons on the first two chapters of the Song.

So while we Western Christians may find it difficult in our time to penetrate the mystery and symbolism of the Song of Songs, it is important to remember that our spiritual ancestors in both Judaism and Christianity have considered it an example of important truth and a great treasury of God's mysteries. It is this fact that makes our study important.

As we move ahead now into these next two lessons, there are two features of this song to keep in mind. These are the two things that readers over the centuries have commented upon since the song was first written and sung in Israel: (1) It has perhaps the loveliest and richest expression of the experience of love between a man and a woman found anywhere in all of literature. Its sentiments have been captured and imitated in more than a thousand songs of people across the world. (2) The language of human love illuminates the character of God's love for us, and of our love for Him. It is because the Song of Songs is a gateway to understanding divine love that it has been so treasured in ancient and medieval times as an allegory of God's love for Israel and of Christ's love for His church.

We must necessarily use common human experience in order to understand the uncommon and divine. This is the route followed by the greatest Hebrew teachers and the most exemplary of Christian saints: Human love, though it is imperfect, carries within it a glimpse of the experience of what C. S. Lewis called the "very" love—true love, the love of God.

The Authorship

The book is introduced with these words, "The Song of Songs, which is Solomon's." Does this mean that Solomon wrote the Song? This was the traditional view. Or does it mean simply that the Song is about Solomon, or of Solomon, or for Solomon? This possibility, at least, can easily be seen in the language itself. Many students of the Song insist that we can say no more than that the song is one composed with Solomon as the chief subject.

Another question that really has to do with authorship is often posed. Is this Song one work that was, from the beginning, intended to be presented as a whole? Or is it several songs that are collected under one title but that had different sources?

As we read the Song, we are likely to have the impression of many loosely connected pieces about a young woman and her lover, who sometimes appears to be a king and at other times is referred to as a shepherd. The loose way in which these pieces come together may indeed support the idea that the Song is a patchwork—many different songs pulled together around the common theme of courtship, romantic love, and marriage.

However, there is something else that we should notice: Certain strong common threads of thought are sustained throughout the poem. The interest in royalty and the continual reference to those things that are symbolic of royal privilege and position are scattered throughout the writing.

The reference to a chorus of maidens, the sensual language, the imagery of the vineyard and the garden are all found throughout the Song. It is these things that strongly suggest that the Song was written to be read as a whole and intended to be seen as one wedding song.

The Tokens of Love (1:2-4)

Remember that the words of this Song are aimed more at the heart than at the head. "May he kiss me with the kisses of his mouth! For your love is sweeter than wine" (1:2, NASB). The images expressed here are physical and sensual. The kiss has, from time immemorial, been a token of personal love, affection, ardor, and great attraction. This imagery is maintained throughout the song—the lover kisses the beloved, draws her to him, and courts her affection in every way possible. He stops at nothing, and nothing escapes his attention. The passions of love in real life wax and wane, but the Song celebrates young love at its peak.

The Strongest Thing in the World

The image reminds us that the strongest thing in the world is love: "for your love is better than wine" (ESV). Indeed, there is nothing that surpasses love, a truth so beautifully expressed by Paul in his first letter to the Christians at Corinth (chapter 13).

Men will give up much for the sake of love. History is full of stories and legends of the worlds that have been conquered and the fortunes that have been lost—all for the sake of love. The long trail of love can be traced from Helen, whose face "launched a thousand ships" in the epic of Homer, to Shakespeare's Juliet, for whom the ardent Romeo would give his life, to the Duke of Windsor, who abdicated the British throne for the woman he loved.

It is no wonder that from the earliest days of this Song the application was made to God's love. We ask, "Does God love with the same ardor? Does He contend for love at a great price?" Now, using this language that aims at the heart, we begin to see something extraordinary about the Old Testament view of God.

Here is no divine abstraction nor aloof deity, complete and sufficient in Himself, who could not be touched by our feelings and emotions. That was the god of Aristotle and the Greek world perhaps, but it was not the God of Israel.

God's Love Knows No Limits

Instead, we see here a God whose love knows no limits, who loves us with a costly love but who does not count the cost. Because of this Song, God has been portrayed in the imagination of people across the centuries as the Lover whose attention to His beloved was too complete and too all-consuming to be disturbed by lesser matters. In the Song we confront a God whose unreserved and relentless love pursues and courts people—a God who doesn't give up on us.

It is true that there are a variety of images of God in our Bible. We see Him as the awesome Creator, as a supreme Judge, as a caring Father, but He is also a Lover. In fact, He is *the* Lover—and we will never know the fullness of love until we give ourselves completely to Him.

Next the Song writer speaks of how "your anointing oils are fragrant" (1:3, ESV). Perfumes of various kinds are used widely today. Advertisers play up the idea that perfume attracts members of the opposite sex. The wearing of perfumes, colognes, and sweet-smelling ointments and oil has always been associated with physical attraction.

"Thy Name Is as Ointment"

The application of this idea to the lover goes even further. "Your name," the poet says, "is perfume poured out" (1:3, AMP). The reference here to "your name" covers far more than a characteristic of a person or a lotion or perfume. Rather, the idea being expressed is that it is the person himself. "Thy name" refers to the person's character.

The name of God is very important in the Old Testament. There were, in fact, several different names for God. Most of them described some characteristic of God. He is God Almighty, *El Shaddai*. He is a God of exceeding nobility and majesty: *Elohim*. And there is a way that God has made Himself known as a personal God. He is a God who is "for us" or "on our side." These ideas are included in the name of God given to Moses at Mount Sinai. It is the four-lettered name, YHWH, which we pronounce as Yahweh, most often translated simply "The Lord," which is the covenant name of God.

The names of God touch on the essence of who He is, and to say who He is, is also to remind ourselves that He is the One without whom we can ever live. His name is an attraction, it calls forth a longing for God. It is "like perfume poured out" (NIV).

The One Who Is Loved (1:5-7)

When a person is in love, they are usually very fastidious about their appearance. Great care goes into looking desirable and attractive. A person in love goes to great lengths to make a good impression.

A Painful Fear

Most of us have had our moments when we've doubted that anyone could possibly be attracted to us. The woman of the Song must have felt this as she seems to reflect a mixture of emotions. On one hand she is delighted that the king loves her. On the other hand, though, she is painfully aware of her defects.

In ancient times to be tanned or sunburned was thought to mar the beauty of a woman. But this rustic maiden in the Song worked outside in the vineyard. "Do not gaze at me," she says, "because I am dark, because the sun has looked upon me" (1:6, ESV). By this she means she is deeply tanned and doesn't have the pampered skin of a young woman of privilege and status.

It is quite easy for most of us to identify with the mixed emotions of a young woman who is pleased that her lover finds her attractive but who at the same time is painfully self-conscious about what she perceives as a noticeable flaw in her beauty. We experience this in our relationship with God. We know that He loves us, and this gives us exhilarating feelings of joy. But at the same time we are flooded with a crippling awareness of the flaws of sin and guilt. Ironically it is God's love that makes us aware of those flaws.

The brilliance and warmth of love make us aware of our flaws in a way that harsh judgment and condemnation never could. Before his vision of God, the prophet Isaiah fell down and declared himself "a man of unclean lips . . . in the midst of a people of unclean lips" (Isaiah 6:5, KJV). Centuries later Peter begged Jesus to "'Go away from me, Lord, for I am a sinful man!'" (Luke 5:8, NASB). Love both delights us, in that we are loved, and appalls us in that we see ourselves as receiving what we do not deserve.

A Desire to Be Alone

Evidently gaining a bit of confidence now, the young woman says, "Tell me, you whom I love, where you graze your flock and where you rest your sheep at midday. Why should I be like a veiled woman beside the flocks of your friends?" (1:7, NIV). While her lover is a king, she is still a country girl at heart. So she shifts now to the idiom of shepherd life, using a pastoral image as a coded way to ask, "Where can I find you when you are alone?"

It is common for two people who are deeply in love to desperately want to be alone. That's how romantic love and friendship differ. Friends enjoy being together at a party where there is fun and conversation. But two people in love want only to be alone together. Romantic love that is authentic, and certainly the kind of love expressed in this Song, is monogamous. As the lyrics of the old love song say, "I only have eyes for you." That is the mood of the young woman in this part of the Song.

One Love, One God

Without straining too much at this point, we get a picture of how this scene is analogous to our relationship with God. Central to the mood of the Jewish religion is the *Shema,* a saying that is repeated by a faithful Jew every morning and every evening: "Hear, O Israel: The LORD our God is one LORD: and thou shalt love the LORD thy God with all thine heart, and with all thy soul, and with all thy might" (Deuteronomy 6:4–5, KJV).

It was this that Jesus quoted as "the most important" commandment. But then He picked up on another Old Testament quotation when He added a second commandment: "Love your neighbor as yourself" (Mark 12:31, NIV). Then Jesus added, "There is no commandment greater than these."

Now we begin to see how romantic love illustrates our idea of one God. The love of God excludes the possibility of putting anyone or anything else in His place. And just as a couple's love can only grow and develop in an environment of faithfulness, so also the love of God demands steadfast loyalty. The message we are getting from the Song here is that the exclusiveness of romantic love mirrors the exclusive love of God.

The Qualities of the Beloved (1:8–11)

As we noted earlier, it is through the warmth of love that we become aware of those things about ourselves that from our point of view seem less attractive. Lovers, male or female, usually feel insecure. There is that within each of us that causes us to feel that our physical or emotional flaws would somehow keep another person—our lover—from really loving and accepting us.

The young woman in the Song had expressed this concern, as we have seen, because of her skin that had been darkened through exposure to the sun. She knew that she was "lovely," but she was still self-conscious about her looks (1:5–6, NIV).

The Fairest Among Women

Now, in response to her feelings, her king-lover expresses colorfully what he sees when he looks at her. He doesn't see the flaw that distresses her. Instead, to him she is the "most beautiful among women" (1:8, ESV). Just as a sculptor finds within a rock or a block of granite a beautiful and flowing form, so the true lover sees beyond the exterior and detects an inward beauty that someone else might not see.

A Colorful and Unique Comparison

Then he becomes profuse as he says, "I liken you, my darling, to a mare among Pharaoh's chariot horses" (1:9, NIV). Now, it isn't likely that any suitor today would draw that kind of comparison, but in ancient times this would be the highest of compliments. The reference is likely to the Egyptian Arabian horses that an Egyptian king would have kept in his stables. Among the most beautiful animals is the Egyptian Arabian horse. The Arabian's flowing lines, gracefully tapered neck, sculpted head, and shapely legs give this breed of horse an elegance, dignity, and beauty that is breathtaking. Indeed, this was a prize above all others.

What His Love Saw

Then in the language of love the king-lover tells the queenly young woman that to him, "Your cheeks are lovely with ornaments, your neck with strings of jewels" (1:10, ESV). He doesn't even see a sun-darkened skin but a beautiful face that is rimmed with rows of jewels and hanging pendants.

Here again, the language of love in the Song speaks to us of God's love. He doesn't see us as we are but as we are born to be. He sees us through "eyes of grace." He loves us with a love that sees beyond external flaws. Instead, with the penetrating eyes of the lover, God sees in us the majesty and character that He has intended for us all along.

The Apostle Paul defined authentic love in these words: Love "believes all things, hopes all things" (1 Corinthians 13:7, NASB).

Love's Environment (1:12–17)

In these next verses of our scripture lesson we listen in on the dialogue between the king-lover and the young woman in the

Song. In these exchanges we gain real insight into the way they think and feel. And as we catch their thinking and feeling we begin to see how the strength and power of their love affects their whole environment. It is what they think of themselves and about each other that mirrors their spirit of love. But even more important, we see how their thinking and feeling affect the way they see and understand the world around them.

The Appeal of the Senses

The setting for this conversation between the lovers is apparently in a secluded spot in a wooded area where the two of them can be alone. The young woman speaks first, and she invokes the image of aroma as she speaks of her lover: "While the king was on his couch, my nard gave forth its fragrance. My beloved is to me a sachet of myrrh that lies between my breasts" (1:12–13, ESV). The reference here is to the aromatic scent of her perfume. Spikenard or "nard" is an aromatic oil that would be used as perfume. Myrrh is resin from an aromatic plant that was collected in a small cloth bag that hung around the neck.

Then as the young woman continues to speak of her king-lover, in addition to the aroma image, she speaks of sight: "My beloved is to me a cluster of henna blossoms from the vineyards of En Gedi" (1:14, NIV). To her he is as handsome and fragrant as the aromatic white blossoms of the cypress or henna flower, which grew prolifically along the coast of Israel and in the Jordan valley. But her reference to the vineyards of En Gedi locates the setting of her mental picture in the beautiful oasis located on the western shore of the Dead Sea.

The Language of Love

The language of two people deeply in love is always rich in metaphor, even today. In these few descriptive words we catch the depth of her feeling of love and devotion.

In verse 15 the king-lover responds by telling her how beautiful she is to him. Then he draws a striking metaphor as he compares her eyes to beautiful doves, and this draws her response: "Behold, you are beautiful, my beloved, truly delightful" (1:16, ESV).

The atmosphere and environment of love completely engulf the lover and his beloved and their wooded setting, which is described symbolically as a house with beams of cedar and rafters of fir (1:17).

Because of their love, wherever they were it was beautiful and perfect. Many married couples will remember their first home or apartment. It may have been only two or three humble rooms and without the amenities that came along later. But to them in their newly married euphoric state, it was heaven!

The Power of Love (2:1–17)

Lovers of all time have expressed their feelings with energy, power, exuberance, and joy. We think and speak extravagantly about the one we love—and that is as it should be. And while this exuberance and extravagance finds different expressions with the passing of time, it is something that should never be lost by a couple whether they are twenty or seventy. How important it is for the spark of love to keep glowing through the changing stages of life!

Energetic Images

As we move now into this next part of our scripture lesson, the feelings and images remain strong and powerful. Note, for example, the young woman's description of her lover: "Listen! My beloved! Look! Here he comes, leaping across the mountains, bounding over the hills" (2:8, NIV). It is spring, winter is past, and he wants her to be with him. This is a marvelous description of a lover. This scene is packed with eagerness and action.

Again, this description is analogous to God's love. He pursues us with energy, boundless enthusiasm, and at an extravagant cost. The Apostle Paul had ample cause to speak of God's love as he did when he wrote to the Christians at Ephesus, "And walk in love, as Christ loved us and gave himself up for us, a fragrant offering" (Ephesians 5:2, ESV). The whole spirit of the gospel centers around the high cost of God's love in Christ for us. No cost, no energy, was spared in our behalf.

Love and Loveliness

A characteristic of love is that it sees the best in the one loved. And when we concentrate on the best, that is what we see. These two lovers in the Song are well aware of this truth. The Plain of Sharon runs from Joppa north to Mount Carmel. There is beauty on the plain, but in drawing descriptive comparisons, the Song writer sees perhaps its most beautiful feature—the "rose of Sharon" (2:1). From what we know of that part of the world, it is likely that the "rose" was actually a colorful crocus that bloomed profusely in season.

Reference is made to "the lily of the valleys"—"the lily among thorns" (2:2, KJV). The king-lover is actually telling his beloved here that her beauty is that of a lily among thorns. And in response to that colorful compliment, our writer has the young woman comparing her lover to "an apple tree among the trees of the forest" (2:3, NASB). In each case we see the eyes of love fixed on the most beautiful—the rose, the lily, and the sweet, fruit-producing apple tree.

The Apostle Paul picked up on this particular virtue of love when he gave this good advice to the Christians at Philippi, "Finally, brethren, whatsoever things are true, whatsoever things are honest, whatsoever things are just, whatsoever things are pure, whatsoever things are lovely, whatsoever things are of good report . . . *think on these things*" (Philippians 4:8, KJV, emphasis added).

There is a powerful lesson of love for Christians in today's world in this whole thought. There is much in our world that is ugly and unpleasant. There are traits in people that are hard at times for us to take. So often it is the bad news that is played up in headlines and on our 24-hour news outlets. But for God's chosen people, these are not the things we are to concentrate on. That doesn't mean that we are blind to what goes on around us. But it does mean that we are to view the world and the people in it through eyes that have been enlightened by God's love.

Love Awakened

The penetrating power of love to see only the lovely invokes a response. Love is communication between two persons, and between God and a person. Love is giving and receiving. In today's vernacular, we would say that love is a "two-way street."

In verses 4 through 7 we have a picture of the overwhelming feelings of two lovers. In verses 4, 5, and 6 the young woman—the beloved, the bride—continues speaking to or about her lover. In verse 5 the King James Version's *flagons* is translated "raisins" or "raisin cakes" in modern versions. But apparently the idea being expressed is that she was so overcome with love that she was refreshed and revived by fruit offered by her lover. The translation of verse 7 is somewhat vague. Some scholars attribute these words to the king-lover and others to the young woman, but in either case, one of the lovers here is so caught up in the beloved's love that he or she is warning others not to disturb them.

The important thing we are getting here is that love involves a response. A woman responds to the man who loves her; a man responds to the woman who loves him. And in their mutual response their love is fully expressed. And the application to us is clear—we are to respond actively to God's love in the very practical and everyday affairs of life. If we fail to do that, His love cannot be fully expressed in and through us.

In verses 8 through 14 the dialogue continues to move back and forth. First, the young woman, with metaphors and poetic beauty, lauds the vigor and grace of her king-lover (2:8–13). She sees him having the strength to leap over mountains and hills with the grace of a young stag or mountain goat. Once again we have the image of spring, of nature coming to life after the winter. Birds are singing, fruit is coming out on the trees. This is the season for love, and they want to be together.

Next, the king speaks again. He speaks endearingly of her as "my dove" and urges her to be with him—in the hills and in the secret places (2:14). There is much in this ancient poem that is obscure for us. But the picture remains clear that here are two people who are extravagantly in love, giving and receiving as God intended.

The Little Foxes

In this euphoric atmosphere of love, the writer seems to inject a note of warning: "Catch the foxes for us, the little foxes that spoil the vineyards, for our vineyards are in blossom" (2:15, ESV). While the true meaning of this saying is a bit obscure, it seems likely that the warning being sounded is to avoid those little things that can be destructive of love.

While love is powerful, it is also fragile and doesn't yield to great pressure or a frontal assault very often. Even as termites can create havoc in a house, very small things—little slights—can be destructive of love. The biting putdown or the rude and thoughtless remark directed toward a spouse may indeed be one of the "little foxes" that can invade and spoil a home. It is not a major career failure, as a rule, that wrecks a relationship, but the failure to communicate, the unwillingness to be vulnerable and discuss an offensive habit, a refusal to really listen, or the neglect of expressing gratitude or being affirming. It is these seeming "little" things that can sour the grapes of love.

In a similar way, it is frequently the "little foxes" that can spoil our relationship with God—the neglect of prayer and Bible study, a failure to confess our sins, laxness in our relationship with fellow Christians and the church, critical attitudes . . . . These are just some of the "little foxes" that can invade our vineyard of zeal for God. Even if we are not guilty of willful or flagrant sin, we still need to be wary of those "little foxes" in our lives that are permitted to nibble away at our faith.

A Search for Love

In these five verses we have a picture of frantic separation. The lover-king is away from his beloved, and she is desperate in her search for him. She seems to be caught up in a paralyzing fear that she has lost him. This fear drives her out into the streets in a frenetic search. Then when she finally found him, she "would not let him go" (3:4, KJV).

The Pursuit of God

As we've already seen, in our study of the Song we have to think along two tracks. On one hand, this is a passionate love poem—it is about romantic love, the love of a man for a woman and the love of a woman for a man.

On the other hand, as a part of our sacred Scriptures, it should tell us something about God and about our relationship to Him. And it does. For we've already had ample opportunity to see the correlation between human romantic love and the love of God.

In chapter 3, verses 1–5, we have watched and listened as this young woman searched frantically for her king and husband. Even though he was away, he filled her thoughts. She could think and talk about nothing but him. And then she launched her search and finally found him and would not let him go.

This is most emphatically a parable of the Christian life. Here is our pattern for the pursuit of God. There is that within us that can't stand the vacuum of His apparent absence. Augustine worded it this way in his *Confessions*: "Thou awakest us to delight in Thy praise; for Thou madest us for Thyself, and our heart is restless, until it repose in Thee."

The energy and motive force of the true spiritual life comes precisely from the feeling that we have not yet arrived; we are constantly "becomers" in our striving to be wholly God's.

Surely our prayer for each day might well be: *Awake within us, O Lord, a holy desire to have fellowship with You, and an unfailing hunger to see You wherever You may be found.*

The Homecoming (3:6-11)

The next scene moves us abruptly into a changing setting. Here we see the young woman being royally escorted to the king's royal city. Here the king is identified as Solomon, and his royal city is Jerusalem. The litter on which she traveled is colorfully described in verses 7 through 10. No detail is omitted.

It is interesting that in verse 6 the young woman is being brought "out of the wilderness." There's a subtle historical reference here that the early Israelites would have picked up. Escorted by the king, the young woman is being brought out of the wilderness just as their ancestors were delivered from bondage after the Exodus and their years "in the wilderness." There's a parallel here, too, with the pillar of fire and the smoke (cloud) that guided the Israelites on their journey. In addition, recreated in this brief poem is the victory over the Canaanites and the occupation of the land and ultimately the occupation of Mount Zion by David and then Solomon.

Having come this far, the next step is easy for us to grasp. At the time of the writing of this Song the people were fully familiar with the escape from Egypt, the dangers of the wilderness wanderings, and the conquest of Canaan. To them this was the story of how God delivers His people. They saw that they might be in bondage because of sin, but God would free them. They knew that their progress from here on in the wilderness might be perilous, but He would protect them and guide them. Their background might be that of enslavement, but God would make them into a great kingdom.

The later prophets and the early church carried the image further. A person is enslaved to sin, but God will save. And for the Christian, salvation through Jesus Christ includes protection and guidance through the wilderness of the world, and in the end, He will bring us to the Zion of eternity with Him.

This is the great Good News of our Christian faith—we have hope for this present life, and that hope stretches ahead in the vast eternity of God. Paul captured this in his letter to Titus when he said, "He saved us, not on the basis of deeds which we did in righteousness, but in accordance with His mercy, by the washing of regeneration and renewing by the Holy Spirit, whom He richly poured out upon us through Jesus Christ our Savior, so that being justified by His grace *we would be made heirs according to the hope of eternal life*" (Titus 3:5–7, NASB, emphasis added).

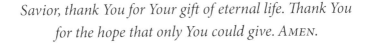

Savior, thank You for Your gift of eternal life. Thank You for the hope that only You could give. AMEN.

For, lo, the winter is past, the rain is over and gone; the flowers appear on the earth.

>   —Song of Songs 2:11–12 (KJV)

Winter had dragged on forever on the East Coast. Boston snowfall toppled all previous records. My hometown, Concord, New Hampshire, endured endless snow that reached halfway up to my daughter's kitchen window. Bone-cracking cold made even the hardiest Granite State natives consider moving to Florida.

Toward the end of April, ponds were still frozen and dirty snow covered dead grass. Drifts of sand, detritus from road deicing, smothered any incipient life, anything green. What had happened to "April showers bring May flowers"? Then, while walking downtown in the thin sunshine, despairing of the bleak landscape, I glimpsed a purple fragment. A tattered trash bag?

I looked closer. Tiny clumps of violets sprouted along the edge of the sidewalk, wedged against a brick apartment building and growing out of matted dead leaves and sand. Apparently, the cement and brick retained just enough warmth from the southern exposure to coax these dainty flowers to bloom despite the blustery weather.

I found myself smiling. These delicate bits of life had broken the gloom. Hope is a funny thing: Just a smidgen can refresh a mood and restore faith. A resilient spirit needs the tiniest of jumpstarts. As I continued my walk, I noticed tiny green threads of grass in the matted dun turf. If I looked closely, I could see half-inch spears of lilies and tulips poking through. I found the crocuses blooming by the library—late, yes, but wonderfully alive.

Spring had been here all along. As soon as I expected to find it, I did.

Lord of all, may we always be mindful of the tiny ways You lead us to great truths.

—Gail Thorell Schilling

Notes

Notes

Notes

LESSON 8: SONG OF SONGS 4-8

Love and Desire: Romantic Love and the Love of God

Savior, I am grateful for Your fulfilling, satisfying love. It fills in all the empty spaces, all the gaps left behind by human loves. AMEN.

In our last lesson on the Song of Songs, we saw how love filled the lover with wonder and admiration for the beloved one. We also were reminded that the lovers' perception of beauty is intensified. Lovers see beauty in each other and in all the world around them. But most especially their attention is focused on each other.

Most of us, at one time or another, have heard someone say, "I just don't know what they see in each other." That is what the writer of the Song is getting at when he has the women in the city say to the young woman, "How is your beloved better than others, most beautiful of women?" (5:9, NIV).

The response, though, to such a question, however it is worded, is always the same. Two people in love see only beauty and loveliness in each other. And now as we continue our study of the Song, we will follow the progress of love as desire is intensified. The temperature of the Song rises. No longer is love being expressed at a distance, for now in poetic language we see and hear love expressed in nearness and intimacy as the young woman asserts with confidence, "I am my beloved's and my beloved is mine; he grazes among the lilies" (6:3, ESV).

We have moved now in the Song from vision to reality, from promise to consummation. In speaking of his own experience in his great expression of love, the Apostle Paul worded it this way: "For now we see through a glass [mirror], darkly; but then face to face" (1 Corinthians 13:12, KJV). What is veiled or unclear now will become clear at the appropriate time. That is where we are in this Song now as interpreted by the language of love.

Beauty and Desire (4:1–5:1)

There is a progression in this part of our scripture lesson comparable to the progression in romantic love that is fulfilled in marriage and consummated in sexual union. First, in colorful and poetic language the king-lover describes the beauty he sees in his beloved (4:1–7). He begins by saying, "How beautiful you are, my darling! Oh, how beautiful!" (4:1, NIV). Then, after describing her beauty (4:1–6), he closes by saying, "You are altogether beautiful, my darling; there is no flaw in you" (4:7, NIV).

Following that glowing description of her beauty, the king-lover becomes intensely aware of his desire for her (4:8–15). In response, the young woman-bride invites him to find his enjoyment and fulfillment in making love (4:16). And finally, the young man responds to her invitation to make love and they enjoy sexual union (5:1).

The Language of the Senses

The language of chapter 4 is sensual. In fact, almost all of the senses are engaged. The poetic, passionate language makes reference to sight or appearance, smell, taste, and hearing or sounds—all of the five senses except touch.

That sense is the last; it waits until the bridal veil is drawn. All of the senses imply touch, but touch, more than the others, implies the full intimacy of the married couple.

Often the senses have been called the "gateways to the mind." We know only what we hear, see, smell, taste, and touch. It is true that often we "sense" intuitively that which we have not actually encountered with the senses. But even then our imagination relates these things to us through the senses. When we think of a possibility we "see" it in our minds. If we feel the need for a vacation at the beach, immediately a stretch of sand pounded by ocean waves and lined by palm trees pops into our minds. We relate to the world through the senses.

Things that are eternal and spiritual, however, do not appear to us quite that way. When we think of heaven we may visualize a spot on Daytona Beach, but we have no way of knowing whether our vision of heaven is at all right. God's love can be stated in an abstract fashion: "For God so loved the world" (John 3:16, KJV), or "Love . . . endureth all things" (1 Corinthians 13:7, KJV). But the Bible does not always state things that way. Instead the writer may draw a picture that appeals to our senses. It is through the picture that our senses—sight, hearing, touch, taste, and smell—enable us to identify with and participate in truth. Nowhere is this appeal to the senses more fully realized than in this Song. And in chapter 4 we are appealed to in every possible way.

Educators who teach children know that the more they appeal to the senses in their young students, the more successful they will be in getting the lesson across. If the student *hears* the lesson, that engages one sense; however, if that student also *sees* something, the teaching is much more effective. But if, in addition, the student is able to touch, or even smell and taste, the impression of the lesson is even stronger.

That's the way it is with this love poem. The lesson is about God's love, and through the poetic language and our imagination, all of our senses are brought into the story.

As we reflect on the mood and the wording in this part of the Song, we can't help but be caught up in the joy and exuberance of the king-lover and his bride. They are completely captivated with each other. There's nothing casual or blasé about their feelings and how they express them. Instead, there is a lively intensity and an earthiness about them that is real.

A Pattern for Marriage

These scenes and the accompanying dialogue give us a pattern for a healthy and fun marriage relationship. The intensity and the openness of the couple in the Song models for us a pattern of marriage that gives it zest and interest. Too often in our "settling down" process we become careless and thoughtless. Once the honeymoon is over, we begin to neglect the niceties that made life attractive and fun. We lose the sense of excitement and anticipation that drew us together, and we become dull and stop trying.

That kind of mood may well be the reason more than half of all marriages end in divorce and havoc rages in the home and family. If the joy, mutual admiration, affirmation, and excitement are freely expressed in marriage at each stage of life, then isn't it more likely that the love that brought a couple together will hold them together?

A Model for Life with God

These scenes and dialogue in this part of the Song give us a model for our relationship to God. This relationship grows and thrives on joy, trust, adoration, praise, and thankfulness. There should be no "settling" down in our relationship with God. To become careless with prayer, praise, Bible study, and serving others is to become cold and indifferent.

Christians Are Meant to Enjoy Life

The Christian life is to be lived in the kind of love and abandon we find expressed here in the Song of Songs. As Christians we are meant to enjoy life to the full—to love God and people and to be able to express that love openly.

Unfortunately, there are those who look and act as if the Christian life is a burden—something to be endured rather than enjoyed. Not only is that attitude defeating to a person with that kind of Christianity, but it discourages others from the way of faith. And besides, that isn't the model of life that Jesus gave us. He was a Person of intensity who felt things strongly. But He wasn't a religious snob—He was comfortable with all kinds of people. And He seemed to enjoy life; He must have been a fun person to be around because more than once we read that the crowds followed Him gladly.

So, when we read, "Eat, friends, and drink; drink your fill of love" (5:1, NIV), we should be reminded that we are to drink deeply of life and of the privilege of living and serving and praying in the presence of God. It is when we truly enjoy God that our life with Him grows and matures.

Love: Pleasure and Pain (5:2-8)

Continuing on his pleasure-of-love theme, the Song writer now introduces us to another scene. The young woman-bride has prepared herself for bed and is asleep when she hears her groom-lover calling at the door. When she became aware that he was at the door her stomach knotted with anticipation and her heart pounded. But by the time she could get dressed and to the door he was gone. Our writer's description of her feeling of pain tells us just how intensely she had been waiting for him.

In verses 6 through 8 we once again see her searching the streets for her husband and lover. In her search she endures pain and misunderstanding (5:7). But she longs for him and needs him so much that she persists and freely admits that she is "faint with love" (5:8, NIV).

This tender scene underscores the pleasure, the pain, and the cost of love between two people who have committed themselves to each other in marriage. There are people today, as there were in Solomon's time, with the distorted idea that life should be just one pleasurable experience after another without those difficult times that are painful. However, a life with meaning and a life of love are not cheap, but the rewards of devotion and faithfulness are rich.

This scene also underscores the relationship between pain and pleasure in the spiritual life. Here, too, we keep trying, consciously or unconsciously, to find a painless and cost-free way to live a Christian life, and we protest those times when the going isn't easy. We complain over the slightest bump in life's road.

In reality, few of us experience real hardship in the pilgrimage of faith—especially when compared with someone like the Apostle Paul. In writing to his friends at Corinth, he spoke of beatings, stonings, imprisonment, of being hungry and cold. He spoke of being "in danger from rivers, in danger from bandits, in danger from my fellow Jews, in danger from Gentiles; in danger in the city, in danger in the country, in danger at sea; and in danger from false believers" (2 Corinthians 11:26, NIV). But then he adds that he would glory in or boast about those things that cause him trouble (2 Corinthians 11:23–30). And in another place the great apostle said that he counted "all things but loss for the excellency of the knowledge of Christ Jesus my Lord: *for whom I have suffered the loss of all things*" (Philippians 3:8, KJV, emphasis added).

The True Vision of Love (5:9–16)

As we move into this part of our scripture lesson, we can't help but be further impressed with the total devotion of these two lovers to each other. In chapter 4 the king-lover graphically describes the way he sees his bride. In a time when monogamy was not closely followed, he had eyes for only one woman.

Now, in response to the impertinent-sounding question "How is your beloved better than others, most beautiful of women?" (5:9, NIV), the bride makes it clear that she is devoted solely to her lover—she has eyes only for *him*. That is the way it is with authentic romantic love—our full attention is given to the one we love. There can be a false exclusiveness to this kind of love, though, that can be detrimental. It gives rise, for instance, to jealousy and envy, and it can breed suspicion. The threat of jealousy is often the immediate cause of all kinds of mistrust and dishonesty.

So the exclusive nature of romance, the desire to have the one we love all to ourselves, doesn't come from wanting to *own* the one we love, or the imposing of a moral standard, but is of itself in the very experience of romantic love. If anything, it is the nature of romance that gives support to the moral standard.

Once again we catch a parallel here to our relationship with God. The exclusiveness of romantic love is mirrored in the exclusive claim of Almighty God on our undivided love. Monotheism, the belief in one God, is not simply a theoretical or intellectual belief—as if the only matter of importance is whether we accept the *idea* that there is one God. Rather, it is a wholehearted commitment that springs from the very core of our being. Those opening words of the Decalogue, "Thou shalt have no other gods before me" (Exodus 20:3, KJV), are imperatives that direct our *wills*, not theory that influences our minds. It is a commitment that channels our love toward this exclusive claim that God has imposed. Like the exclusive claim on each other by a husband and wife, belief in one God is something to live by, not just something to think about.

We are reminded again through the words in these verses about the way love interprets what we "see." The lover sees the beloved through "rose-colored glasses." We jokingly say that "love is blind." But is it really blind or does it enable us to see the one we love as he or she really is? We see it because it is *there*, not just because we have imagined it. This simply means that love allows us to see accurately and faithfully what others cannot see because their vision has not been energized by love.

In her description of her king-lover the bride colorfully pictures what she sees (5:10–16, NIV). He is "outstanding among ten thousand. His head is purest gold; his hair is wavy and black as a raven. His eyes are like doves. . . . His cheeks are like beds of spice yielding perfume. His lips are like lilies dripping with myrrh. His arms are rods of gold set with topaz. His body is like polished ivory. . . . His legs are pillars of marble. . . . His mouth is sweetness itself; he is altogether lovely." Yes, she sees him as no one else can because, as she says, "This is my beloved, this is my friend, daughters of Jerusalem." She sees him not only as her lover but also as *her friend*.

It is true that these descriptions are lavish, but in so being, they model God's attitude toward us. As His creation, as Christian believers, imperfect as we are, He sees us, in Christ, as possessing those qualities that He affirms and loves. It is true that of ourselves we don't deserve His lavish love, but by His grace, He loves us.

Authentic romantic and family love seeks out and finds those qualities that are worthy of love. As His creation God sees in everyone that which is worthy of love, and through Christ we experience that transforming love and gain a fresh vision of who and what we are in Him.

God's Love and the Church (6:1–9)

In this part of our scripture lesson we have a reaffirmation of the lovers' devotion to each other (6:1–3), and then follows a second description of the bride as her king-lover sees her (6:4–9). As is true throughout this entire Song, this is primarily a love poem. However, throughout the Christian era, as we have already noted, the application has also been made to God's love for individual people and to His love for the church. And in this part of our lesson now many interpreters of Scripture see these words applying to God and His church. Let's take a closer look from this perspective.

In response to her companions' question, "Where has your beloved gone, O most beautiful among women?" (6:1, ESV), the bride in verse 2 tells them precisely where her king-lover is. In relating this to the traditional application of the Song, we can say that while others search for God, not knowing for certain where to find Him, the church, as the body of Christ, knows where He can be found simply because the church belongs in a unique way to God—as a bride belongs to the bridegroom and as he belongs to her (6:3).

The Beauty of the Bride and the Church

Next, as we move through the description of the bride as seen by the king, we catch a parallel to the awesome beauty of the church. In verse 4 the king says, "'You are as beautiful as Tirzah, my darling, as lovely as Jerusalem, *as majestic as an army with banners!*'" (AMP, emphasis added). Here, the bride—and for many Christians the church—is compared to two beautiful cities in Israel's history. Tirzah refers to the first capital of the Northern Kingdom of Israel—a beautiful fortified city in the central hill country. Jerusalem, of course, was the essence of beauty to the ancient Israelites. In speaking of Jerusalem the writer of the book of Lamentations said the city was the "perfection of beauty, the joy of the whole earth" (Lamentations 2:15, KJV).

This, along with the description that follows, is a marvelous love tribute (6:4–9). Here is a commoner who saw herself as a dark-skinned woman of the country enjoying the regal wonders of her king-husband's household. She who saw herself as having flaws is being praised for her beauty and revered for her rank and splendor—"as majestic as an army with banners!" (6:4, AMP).

Ordinary People Make Up the Church

Christian saints over the centuries since the founding of the church have described it as being "as majestic as an army with banners." Majestic? "Awesome," as some other translations render it? What amazing irony, when we stop to consider the makeup of the everyday churches in our own towns or cities. In our time the church is made up of everyday people—the schoolteacher who runs marathons in her spare time, the lift-truck driver who is getting back on his feet after being unemployed for a year, the overachieving business owner who worked his way through several marriages before reaching forty, and the single mom who is scratching out a meager living as an administrative assistant. The church is made up of very human people with human failings and human virtues.

But what does God see in these ordinary people on their struggling pilgrimage? Through the eyes of divine love He sees redeemed royalty. He sees them as they are through Christ, "majestic as an army with banners."

When we pass a jewelry store window and catch sight of a beautifully cut diamond that sparkles with a blinding radiance, there is no similarity to the crude, irregularly shaped rock that was taken from the ground. But in the hands of a skilled diamond cutter that crude rock becomes a gem of startling beauty.

The analogy is obvious. Ordinary, flawed human beings, when shaped by the hand of God, become, by His grace, people of worth and true splendor. If the church is majestic and awesome, it is not because of anything we've done but by His amazing, transforming grace!

God's Love Is Intense and Personal

Let's take it a step further. In verse 9 the king says, "[M]y dove, my perfect one, is unique, the only daughter of her mother, the favorite of the one who bore her. The young women saw her and called her blessed; the queens and concubines praised her" (NIV). In this romantic expression of the king's love for his bride, we are reminded of God's love for us and the church. It was Augustine who said that God loves each of us as if there were only one of us to love. God's love for us is that intense and personal. Dietrich Bonhoeffer, the German pastor and theologian who was martyred toward the end of World War II, said that only in Christ do we truly become individuals. Part of what he meant by that statement comes through in this idea that God's love, like romantic love, is always intense and personal.

The Humility of Love (6:10–13)

In the Apostle Paul's marvelous essay on love he speaks of several of the qualities of love (1 Corinthians 13). Among them is humility. He worded it this way: "Love does not brag and is not proud or arrogant" (1 Corinthians 13:4, AMP). It is this quality of humility that characterizes the attitude and demeanor of the bride-queen.

In verse 9 we saw that the bride was admired for her beauty by the other women in the king's court. Now in verse 10 the description is further enhanced by these words: "Who is this who looks down like the dawn, beautiful as the moon, bright as the sun, awesome as an army with banners?" (verse 10, ESV). And with all of this lavish description we now pick up further indication of how the bride continues to see herself: "I went down to the grove of nut trees to look at the new growth in the valley, to see if the vines had budded or the pomegranates were in bloom" (6:11, NIV). If we were describing her today, we would say, "She is well grounded." Her rural and country background still prompt her thinking and actions in spite of her new position. And we catch a hint in verse 12 that she is scarcely aware of and surprised by ("Before I was aware," NASB) her elevated, queenly status among the people.

An Important Principle
As we reflect on these scenes, a vitally important principle emerges. We see that being loved by God and included as one of His chosen people is something that the Lord does and is not the result of anything we have done or can do. We are like the bride in the Song; we have been elevated to a status we may be scarcely aware of only because of the Lord's love.

This same principle can also be stated in another way. Our place in God's kingdom—His great new society of Christians—is not achieved through our striving, but by humility. It is not by assuming too much or by doing something well that we gain acceptance.

A story is told of two painters who were striving to master their art. One said to himself, *I will become a great painter like Leonardo da Vinci, and everyone will know and admire my paintings.* But he focused so hard on what he would be and what he would gain and how famous he would become that he never mastered the hard work of really learning to paint.

The other painter worked with the idea of doing the best he could. He was content to work hard and remain obscure. Soon the word got around the art world that he was a superb craftsman, and his paintings were in demand. Consequently, he did become well-known and was celebrated as a fine artist.

The difference between these two painters illustrates vividly the power of humility. The first painter didn't so much want to paint as he wanted to be known as a painter—so he failed on both counts. The second painter was oblivious to publicity; he only wanted to paint well. He was a prime example of authentic humility, and this attitude was reflected in his work. For the Christian, humility is the way to spiritual growth.

A Reward of Humility

We also learn here that our Christian character and witness emerges out of a humble spirit. It was because of this spirit that the women in the king's court recognized and praised the queen-bride's beauty and sought out her company. "Return, return, O Shulammite, return, return, that we may look upon you" (6:13, ESV). As with the queen-bride, our attractiveness as Christians and the winsomeness of our faith depends on the sincerity of our witness, which is always the result of authentic humility.

A Third Description of the Bride as the King Saw Her (7:1–9)

Twice before, the king has given elaborate descriptions of his bride. Now, beginning with her feet and legs and moving upward, he gives description after sensual description of her physical charms. The metaphors are rich in Near East color and imagery. Partway through this heady description, the king, in apparent ecstasy, says, "How beautiful and how delightful you are, My love, with all your delights!" (7:6 NASB).

The Hebrew people had a healthy attitude toward sexual pleasure. Within marriage, sex was to be enjoyed, and this is why it was celebrated in their songs and poetry of marriage. For the people of Israel, sexuality was not a *problem* to be lived with, as it was and is in many cultures then and now. Rather, sex was considered a privilege within the covenant of marriage.

Love What Belongs to the One Loved (7:10-13)

The meaning of this next section will come clear as we look at verse 10, "I am my beloved's, and his desire is toward me" (KJV). We've already seen that the king had a passionate sexual desire for his bride. But now we begin to see that his love goes way beyond that. It includes all that she is or has been and it includes those things that she enjoys.

In these verses we see the bride asking her beloved to go with her out to the fields and villages, places familiar to her (7:11–13). She was eager for him to enjoy and be interested in those things that she enjoyed. We all long for our loved ones to participate in those things we enjoy.

Actually, marriage and sexuality take on their character and meaning within the largeness of a life that is united wholly with another person. When a Christian marries, he or she doesn't make a contract only for a physical union or for financial considerations. Instead, we are wholly united. What belongs to one spouse—interests, talents, tastes, background, family, material possessions—becomes, in a way, the spouse's too.

Learning to Love (8:1-4)

On the surface the opening words of our scripture for this section seem strange: "If only you were to me like a brother" (8:1, NIV). She wants to be able to show and express her love openly. She could do this to a brother relative, but she didn't feel free to express her love toward the king in public. That would be inappropriate and would invite criticism.

It is part of learning to love when we are able to express our love and affection in front of other people. This is what the queen-bride wanted to be able to do—she wanted everybody to know that she was passionately in love with the king. There is something very special about a married couple that feels free and relaxed about showing their love and affection publicly in a way that lets everyone know of their commitment to each other.

An Outward Expression of Love

As so often happens in the Song, there's a Christian application to what the queen-bride expresses in verse 1 of our scripture lesson. Jesus taught His disciples to confess Him—to give public witness to their faith in Him. In fact, Jesus attached a special promise to this when He said, "Whoever *acknowledges me before others*, I will also acknowledge before my Father in heaven" (Matthew 10:32, NIV, emphasis added).

As we grow in our love for Christ, we will express our love for Him wherever we are—at work and at play, as well as at home and at church. Our growing love for the Lord will have expression in every part of life. As the familiar song says, "They will know we are Christians by our love." And that love is expressed by both our words and our actions.

Loving to Learn

In verse 2 of this part of our lesson, we catch a hint of something else that is involved in learning to love. The king, widely known for his wisdom, is invited by his bride to be her teacher. She was eager to learn, and there can be no question but that wisdom and learning require an emotional commitment. To really learn, we need to feel a powerful love for learning.

The great artist Henri Matisse once said that sincerity, a sincere desire to pursue his art, was the secret of his genius. Sir Laurence Olivier, gifted actor of stage and screen, insisted that to act well a person had to have a deep desire and love for acting. Yes, love requires learning to love, but learning also requires loving to learn. To achieve the best, we must have an insatiable desire for the best.

Do Not Disturb

Next we have a repeat (8:3–4) of the refrain we heard earlier (2:6–7; 3:5). So intense is her king-lover's love for her and interest in her that she asks the "daughters of Jerusalem" not to interfere with or disturb them. As we've seen through the entire Song, the intensity and energy of love is celebrated. It is an energy that can move us up to wisdom, learning, industry, and every good thing. Love, as the Apostle Paul pointed out, never fails (1 Corinthians 13:8).

Love and Faithfulness (8:5–7)

The scene shifts now to the country home of the bride's mother. This is a touching scene. The bride had come to feel comfortable and at home in the king's palace. Now we see him comfortable and at home in the bride's former surroundings.

Again the symbolism takes shape. The promise that is ours in Christ is an eternal home with Him. This is what the writer of the book of Hebrews meant when he spoke of "the promise of eternal inheritance" (Hebrews 9:15, KJV). But the Lord gave us another promise. He will be with us now where we are—in our homes, in our places of work, wherever we are and whatever we are doing. Jesus assured His disciples of every century and every place that "behold, I am with you always, to the end of the age" (Matthew 28:20, ESV).

But there's more. These verses imply that in the relationship between the king and his bride there is the guarantee of faithfulness. That is the meaning behind these words: "Set me as a seal upon your heart, as a seal upon your arm. . . . Many waters cannot quench love, neither can floods drown it. If a man offered for love all the wealth of his house, he would be utterly despised" (8:6–7, ESV).

Like the love described in these words, God's love is faithful and everlasting—nothing can overcome it. The biblical writers of both the Old and New Testaments were unanimous in stressing this truth about God's love. They were acutely aware of the seriousness of sin and the threat of God's judgment, but what seemed to strike all of them most forcibly was the stubbornness and persistence of God's compassion. God's persistent and stubborn compassion includes everyone!

The Song of Songs, once again, impresses us with the persistence of God's love. He is not easily put off or discouraged—either by our own lack of hope and faith or even by our inclination toward sin. Like the love of the king for his bride and her love for him, the strength of love is greater than even death and the grave (8:6).

Love and Chastity (8:8-13)

This part of our scripture lesson is difficult to understand without some insight into the culture of ancient Israel. There, as in most of the Near East, the entire family had an interest in protecting the chastity of a daughter in the family. When she was presented to her bridegroom on their wedding night, she was to be "undefiled"—a virgin. Her brothers within the family were especially involved in protecting their sister so that her honor and that of the family was preserved.

Many interpreters of the Song see these verses as a testimony of the faithfulness of the bride's brothers, from young girlhood to maturity, in protecting their sister (8:8–10). Her chastity had been carefully preserved through the care of her family.

Then she makes reference to the king and the way he cares for his vineyards (8:11–13). He is a good steward of all that he has. But she reminds him that she, too, has remained in possession of her "vineyard": "My own vineyard is mine to give" (verse 12, NIV). She came to him chaste, and she belongs only to him.

The Bible rates sexual discipline as extremely important. Sex was to be enjoyed only in marriage. Disregard for this eternal principle has resulted in disordered families, fractured relationships, psychological hardships, disease, and even death.

On the other hand, those who restrict physical intimacy to the marriage relationship can experience a depth of love that transcends everything else and can build toward a lasting relationship.

The Longing Heart (8:14)

The last verse of the Song, "Make haste, my beloved, and be thou like to a roe or to a young hart [a gazelle or a goat or a stag] upon the mountains of spices" (8:14, KJV), is an invitation. It speaks of the bride's readiness, willingness, and longing for him.

In the conclusion of this amazing love-poem, we have a picture of the people of God waiting and longing for the presence of Christ. The people of ancient Israel saw themselves as waiting for the coming of the Messiah and the establishment of His kingdom.

The term the "longing heart" is a great theme of our relationship to God. We long for His constant presence in the daily routines of life that involve our hurts and our fears as well as our joys and victories. We long for His presence in our insecurities—in the pain of living and dying. And we long for Him in the anticipation of future life in the spirit of the writer of almost the last words in our sacred Scriptures: "Even so, come, Lord Jesus" (Revelation 22:20, KJV).

Jesus, everything I need for this life is in You.
You give me everything I need. Amen.

> **Place me like a seal over your heart, like a seal on your arm; for love is as strong as death. . . . Many waters cannot quench love, rivers cannot sweep it away.**
>
> —Song of Songs 8:6–7 (NIV)

I knew that my daughter Rebecca and grandson Mark talked often with my husband, Don, during his last days, but I didn't know they recorded an interview. Love was the main topic, and they shared Don's words with me shortly before Christmas. "Love is a big word," he'd said. "You can't define most of what love is. You just love." He paused, then added, "Love always ends in tears."

  We've shed rivers of tears in the months since Don's passing. Each of us has taken comfort in a different way. My granddaughter Olivia grew cuttings from his plants in the windowsill of her apartment. Rebecca had one of Don's suit jackets cut down to fit her and wears it often. My grandson Caden learned how to weld using Don's farm welder. Sons and grandchildren called often to share favorite stories. I've kept Don's watch and glasses on the bedroom dresser, and his collection of farm caps still decorates the coat tree.

Love is indeed a big word, and Don was right: It always ends in tears. But I've come to understand that sorrow is a necessary and valuable part of love. And I cling to the promise in Revelation 21:4 (NIV): "He will wipe every tear from their eyes. There will be no more death or mourning or crying or pain, for the old order of things has passed away."

Eternal Savior, thank You for tears and memories, for actions that comfort, and especially for Your deep and abiding love that heals our hearts.

—Penney Schwab

Notes

Notes

Notes

Acknowledgments

Every attempt has been made to credit the sources of copyrighted material used in this book. If any such acknowledgment has been inadvertently omitted or miscredited, receipt of such information would be appreciated.

Scripture quotations marked (AMP) are taken from the *Amplified Bible*. Copyright © 2015 by The Lockman Foundation, La Habra, California. All rights reserved.

Scripture quotations marked (ESV) are taken from *The Holy Bible, English Standard Version*. Copyright © 2001 by Crossway Bibles, a division of Good News Publishers. Used by permission. All rights reserved.

Scripture quotations marked (KJV) are taken from the *King James Version of the Bible*.

Scripture quotations marked (NASB) are taken from the *New American Standard Bible*®, Copyright © 1960, 1971, 1977, 1995, 2020 by The Lockman Foundation. All rights reserved.

Scripture quotations marked (NIV) are taken from *The Holy Bible, New International Version*®, *NIV*®. Copyright © 1973, 1978, 1984, 2011 by Biblica, Inc. Used by permission. All rights reserved worldwide.

A Note from the Editors

We hope you enjoyed *Living with Purpose Bible Study: Proverbs, Ecclesiastes & Song of Songs,* published by Guideposts. For over 75 years, Guideposts, a nonprofit organization, has been driven by a vision of a world filled with hope. We aspire to be the voice of a trusted friend, a friend who makes you feel more hopeful and connected.

By making a purchase from Guideposts, you join our community in touching millions of lives, inspiring them to believe that all things are possible through faith, hope, and prayer. Your continued support allows us to provide uplifting resources to those in need. Whether through our communities, websites, apps, or publications, we inspire our audiences, bring them together, and comfort, uplift, entertain, and guide them. Visit us at guideposts.org to learn more.

We would love to hear from you. Write us at Guideposts, P.O. Box 5815, Harlan, Iowa 51593 or call us at (800) 932-2145. Did you love *Living with Purpose Bible Study: Proverbs, Ecclesiastes & Song of Songs*? Leave a review for this product on guideposts.org/shop. Your feedback helps others in our community find relevant products.

Find inspiration, find faith, find Guideposts.

Shop our best sellers and favorites at
guideposts.org/shop

Or scan the QR code to go directly to our Shop

Printed in the United States
by Baker & Taylor Publisher Services